From Roots to Roses

From Roots to Roses

The Autobiography of Tilda Kemplen

TRANSCRIBED AND EDITED BY

NANCY HERZBERG

The University of Georgia Press

ATHENS & LONDON

© 1992 by Tilda Kemplen
All rights reserved
Published by the University of Georgia Press
Athens, Georgia 30602
Designed by Kathi L. Dailey
Set in Berkeley Old Style by
Tseng Information Systems, Inc.
Printed and bound by Thomson-Shore, Inc.
The paper in this book meets the guidelines for
permanence and durability of the Committee on
Production Guidelines for Book Longevity of the
Council on Library Resources.

Printed in the United States of America

96   95   94   93   92   C   5   4   3   2   1

Library of Congress Cataloging in Publication Data

Kemplen, Tilda.
    From roots to roses : the autobiography of Tilda
Kemplen / transcribed and edited by Nancy Herzberg.
       p.   cm.
    ISBN 0-8203-1412-9 (alk. paper)
    1. Kemplen, Tilda.   2. Volunteer workers in social
service—Tennessee, East—Biography.   3. Child care
workers—Tennessee, East—Biography.   4. Volunteer
workers in community development—Tennessee,
East—Biography.   I. Herzberg, Nancy.   II. Title.
HV40.32.K46A3   1992
362.7′092—dc20
[B]   91-26623
                                                    CIP

British Library Cataloging in Publication Data available

This book is dedicated to my wonderful family in recognition of their love, patience, understanding, and support: my son, Ralph; and my daughter, Chris; my daughter-in-law, Betty; each of my six grandchildren, Jami, Brenden, Daniel, Michael, Tammy, and James, who have brought my life new meaning and made me more determined to write this book as a token of my love and appreciation for my family; my late husband, James Kemplen, who supported me in my work and encouraged me to continue; my late parents, Arthur Lee Guy and Nancy Siler Guy, who helped me learn about God, life, and nature; my brother, sisters, nieces, and nephews. This book is also dedicated to members of my staff, who have helped me through good times and bad, and to Nancy Herzberg, for her inspiration, encouragement, and hard work—and waiting while I went on working with people and ignoring the work on the book.

Contents

Preface

In this book, Tilda Kemplen tells the inspiring story of her life, one filled with tireless service to the people of her area. She is the founder and director of Mountain Communities Child Care and Development Centers, Inc., which operates the only child care center for families in Tennessee's rugged and sparsely populated mountains of Campbell County and neighboring Claiborne County. Through years of teaching and organizing, her vision, hopes, and aspirations have become part of the lives of many, both in the communities in which she works and throughout central Appalachia. Hers is a story of dreams becoming reality in the midst of hardship and struggle.

Tilda is native to the Clear Fork Valley of East Tennessee, near the Kentucky border. She lives in rural Campbell County, between White Oak and Clairfield, Tennessee, on top of a hill bordered by Roses Creek Hollow and King Branch Hollow. Local people call this hill "Varmint County." The small communities in this area are isolated by the natural barriers of mountains and narrow, winding roads. The streams are polluted from coal mining operations, and stark, treeless stretches are the scars remaining from strip mining in these beautiful, wooded hills. Much of the coal is gone now, and the jobs and many of the people have gone with it. Unemployment soars as high as 75 percent, and most of the families live below the poverty level. A high percentage of adults have less than an eighth-grade education.

This book recounts the story of Tilda's life work in this area and the philosophy behind it. The book grew from a conversation in 1974, the year I left my position as a paralegal with the East Tennessee Research Corporation. In this capacity, I had helped Tilda with the incorporation of her organization. Tilda told me that she would like me to help her write an autobiography someday, but that because we were both so busy, we probably would never settle down to that task. During the years that followed, we communicated only a few times. In 1986, while living in Downeast Maine, I called to ask whether she would still like to pursue work on her book. She said she had just bought a tape recorder to do so.

In the fall of 1987, I spent two months with Tilda taping a series of conversations in front of her fireplace, in the car on the way to an Indian powwow, and on walks in the woods. We often worked on the book after Tilda's long work days, which didn't end when she arrived home. Our interviews were interrupted by the frequent phone calls and visits from friends, family, and coworkers, who are always a part of Tilda's life. We edited the transcribed manuscript during the following three years. Between two further visits, Tilda and I communicated by phone, mail, and package service. The distance between Maine and Tennessee was bridged by our mutual commitment to Tilda's story. The ease of our collaboration may in part stem from the fact that we share a common date of birth, March 23.

The book is composed of four chapters. In the first, Tilda recounts her early years and the fulfillment of her childhood dream of becoming a teacher. Her given name is Matilda; her friends call her "Tilda." She grew up in an extended family, in which her parents shared whatever they had with relatives and friends. Tilda says that most other Appalachian families lived this way. While her father was a coal miner and union man, most of the time her family did not live in a coal mining camp, so they maintained their self-sufficiency, growing their own food and going to their own church. Tilda attended a one-room school that was an integral part of the community, as did most other boys and girls growing up in the mountains in the 1920s and 1930s. She was unable to attend high school due to geographic isolation.

In 1958 at age thirty-two, while raising two children and still living in the mountains, she returned to school to earn her Bachelor of Science in elementary education. During World War II, many women with high school diplomas had filled teaching positions. After the war, they went to college to become better qualified. While Tilda was part of this trend, what made her unusual was that she began college without her high school diploma and had to travel many miles through the mountains to attend. She also applied her training in a unique way. Dissatisfied with the way children with special needs were handled in the school system, she went on for further training in special education and established a special education program in her school.

As recounted in Chapter 2, she did not stop there. Tilda has always held a strong conviction that children are our most precious resource. She was distressed that children of the area were entering school with inadequate social skills and intellectual capabilities. She could see that this situation stemmed from children being "environmentally deprived" because they lived in geographically isolated areas with little chance to mingle with other children. The developmental process was hindered because of limited opportunities to receive the necessary stimulation in early childhood through education and recreation, as well as proper nutrition. In the late 1960s, while still teaching elementary school, Tilda began to organize concerned parents to work to help themselves, their children, and other families in the area by developing a program to begin the educational process at a younger age.

In 1973 she and those community people incorporated a nonprofit organization, Mountain Communities Child Care and Development Centers (MCCCDC) and established a child care and development center. The program began with a single-wide trailer serving a handful of children. It now is housed in a building and serves as many as sixty-two children from infancy to age six. In response to other community needs, MCCCDC has established an impressive array of services, including a Maternal and Infant Health Outreach Worker Program, a toddler outreach program, child abuse and substance abuse prevention programs, food and clothing programs, and adult education and economic development projects. In addition to serving people, MCCCDC has provided employment for a significant number of women, men, and young people.

With her drive and initiative, Tilda has persevered in a region where many leave or resign themselves to the way things are, where many have fallen into hopelessness and despair. While others have gotten their education and left the region, Tilda chose to stay and work to improve the lives of those she loves: her family, her neighbors, and all the members of the mountain communities in the area. Through the programs of MCCCDC, Tilda has helped rebuild the sense of community that had been eroded over the years.

Much of the land in the area is owned by large, absentee landholding corporations that have leased it to mining companies. When people lived in coal company towns, they relied on the companies rather than on themselves to meet their needs. When deep mining began to dwindle and was replaced in large part by strip mining, the people became divided against themselves, deep miners versus strippers.

Not only were people cut off from each other, but they were also cut off from the land. During the coal camp days, they relied on company stores instead of their own gardens. When mechanized deep mining and later when strip mining came in, many jobs were lost. People had a difficult time finding affordable housing and had to move around a lot as they fell on hard times; their ties to home and land were disrupted.

It is in this environment that Tilda has worked to reunite people by helping to organize them to meet their own and one another's needs. She has worked to reestablish people's connection to the land through gardening and small-farms programs, a livestock project, and Native Herb Products, which has also helped reconnect people to their American Indian heritage. She has worked to overcome the divisions among people by emphasizing what unites people: their common humanity expressed in concern for all children and for the community as a whole. All these efforts not only survived but flourished from the late 1960s through to the present, despite diminishing resources to support nonprofit organizations. This work is a tribute to Tilda's clear and unwavering vision of what life in the mountains can be. Through their involvement with MCCCDC projects, many community people have come to share Tilda's vision of a healthier way of life through people helping people.

Chapter 3 deals with Tilda's personal life. She talks about a number of illnesses she has endured while trying to continue her work. While many do not recover from these illnesses, including aplastic anemia and Legionnaires' disease, she survived, due in large part to her positive attitude and faith. She has acted as her own advocate in dealing with the health care system and has done what she could to take charge of her own health. She sensed that she needed to get well in order to continue with her life's mission.

While much of Tilda's energy has gone toward community work, she cares deeply about her family and friends, whom she describes in the section on relationships and home. She herself lives in the kind of extended-family setting in which she grew up. Her son's house is next door, and her daughter lives right across the road. Her children, grandchildren, and neighbors are continually dropping by, calling on the phone, bringing over garden produce, inviting her to supper. She has faced a number of family tragedies besides her illnesses: the death of one of her babies, the death of her husband from black lung disease, the death of her brother soon after a fire took their house. Along with the sustenance she gets from her strong ties to people and to the mountains in which she lives, her love of life, optimism, and sense of purpose have seen her through. According to Tilda, "You're either a worrier or a warrior."

One motivation for pulling through her illnesses was her desire to write this account of her life and work. With this book she wants to help shatter stereotypes that many have held regarding those who live in the Appalachian mountains. Her life is an example of the strength, courage, intelligence, and determination of the region's people. In recognition of her community development work, Tilda was chosen out of thirty-three thousand nominees as one of the five 1980 Jefferson Award winners; this award is presented by the National Institute for Public Service for "outstanding public service benefiting local communities." In 1986, she was chosen by *Ms.* magazine to present Dolly Parton with a Woman of the Year award, since both she and Dolly are natives of East Tennessee who have worked to improve employment opportunities for people of the region.

The final chapter, entitled "From Roots to Roses," describes Tilda's philosophy that community change comes about by encouraging people to find their own potential and by nurturing the talents that each person brings to community endeavors. She talks about the importance of having a vision to guide the work and the importance of commitment to that vision in the face of many obstacles. As she has said, she might not have started anything had she known in advance all that would be involved. Her motto is: "Do it. Even if it turns out wrong, you can learn by it, and the next time you'll do it right." She believes that people can do anything if they believe in themselves. She believes that people who have roots in their heritage can grow into the fulfilled people they were meant to be.

Nancy Herzberg

Acknowledgments

We wish to thank all the people who have provided suggestions, support, and nurture for the writing of *From Roots to Roses*. So many loving hands have guided us along the way that we have been profoundly reminded that we are all connected to one another and need each other to carry out our work. Although we cannot name all who helped, we deeply appreciate everyone who assisted us.

We especially thank Tilda's family and the people of her community, who provided encouragement, and the staff of Mountain Communities Child Care and Development Centers, Inc., who gave their total support. We also give thanks to Nancy Herzberg's family and friends for their help. We particularly want to acknowledge Chuck and Nancy Maland, who opened many doors, including those of their home in Knoxville, Tennessee, and Mark Elsner, who provided editorial assistance and was the first person to read the manuscript and affirm its value. We also thank Don Perryman and Larry Herzberg for their editorial suggestions.

We thank the University of Georgia Press for the professional and caring way they have handled this book's publication. We especially wish to thank Malcolm Call, director of the press.

Several organizations and individuals deserve special mention, as they provided the necessary elements for the writing process to go forward. Research grants were provided by Berea College's Appalachian Center; our thanks go to Loyal Jones, director, and the Appalachian Studies Fellowship Committee. The University of Tennessee-Knoxville provided invaluable assistance. Jack Reese, who was chancellor at the time we were transcribing our audiotapes, agreed to make a computer available to us in an office staffed by Diane Garrett, which she generously shared. The University of Tennessee Press was a vital part of the publishing process. Cynthia Maude-Gembler, then acquisitions editor, gave us encouragement and helpful suggestions. Carol Wallace Orr, then director of the press, and the manuscript readers, John Gaventa, Greer Litton Fox, and Sally Maggard, helped shepherd the manuscript in the right direction. Most of the editing work was completed while Nancy worked at the University of New England in Biddeford, Maine, where Michael Morris, the academic dean of the College of Arts and Sciences, gave his support.

Finally, we give thanks to the Great Spirit, who put people and resources in our path when we needed them and who continues to guide us.

With love,

Tilda Kemplen and Nancy Herzberg

One

My Roots

In the spring of 1925, my family was living in Guy Hollow, a hollow way back in the mountains about two miles from where I now live that was named for my grandfather, John Payton Guy. He had lived there and raised my father and his brothers and sisters in a log cabin. I don't know who built it, but it was one of the older log cabins in the country where my family lived. The logs were put together with wooden pegs; no nails were used. The roof was a board roof; I don't know if it had nails or not. It was a beautiful one-room log cabin. It sat in a beautiful little meadow with hills on both sides and a creek running down on one side.

My mother, Nancy Siler Guy, always told of the blazing beauty of the dogwood blossoms mingled with the redbud blossoms and tiny green leaves peeping out on the trees. Under the trees was a beautiful carpet of wildflowers waking from a long winter's rest, every sign of spring, every sign of God's creation and the resurrection. Along the creeks were blue violets. Yellow daffodils grew in the yards, swaying and dancing in the March wind. In her garden my mother had the most beautiful peas, bursting with beautiful purple blossoms. The day before I was born, her table was dressed with a fresh salad of lettuce and onions from her garden.

From left: Tilda's grandfather, Van Bloom Siler; her uncle, Floyd Siler; and her mother, Nancy Myrtle Siler, at age eighteen

From left: Tilda's Aunt Laura, her mother, and her father, Arthur Guy

My mother was taking care of her garden and her two stepchildren, Thomas and Alene Guy. They were twins, then four years old. Everybody waited anxiously for a baby to be born. On March 23, 1925, about two o'clock in the morning, that baby was born, and that baby was me. Now I needed a name. My mother and father each had a sister named Lucinda; both had died early in life, so they wanted to name me Lucinda. My mother's mother was named Matilda. She died when my mother was a four-year-old child, and my mother wanted me to have her mother's name. So they decided to call me after my grandmother Matilda and my two aunt Lucindas. I never cared for those names when I was growing up, because they were awfully big names. I didn't understand why they gave me those long names, which I had to carry all through school.

As I grew older, I came to like those names, but I didn't know what either name meant until my granddaughter looked in a book about naming babies. She said, "Granny, I looked up your name. Do you know what it means? Matilda means courageous, and Lucinda means brilliant."

I was really happy that my mother and daddy chose those names for me. I don't think they knew what they meant. They just wanted me to be named for their sisters and for my grandmother.

My father, Arthur, worked in the mines, and he trudged across the hills and valleys to work in the Eagan Mine about five miles from where we lived. When his day's work was over, he would draw out his scrip and trade it for groceries at the company store. He carried the groceries home on his back, because the only transportation he had was walking. My father was a coal miner from the time he was eleven until he was sixty-five years old.

We stayed in Guy Hollow in our little log cabin I guess until I was about four years old. Then we moved away to Harlan County, Kentucky, for two years, the only time we ever lived in a coal camp. My father got out of work in Tennessee, and that's why he and others went to Harlan County. The unions were being organized, and my father was a union man. He got a job there, but he couldn't stay long, because if it had been known that he was a union man, he would have been killed.

That time in Harlan County was a bloody time. My mother said that in those days she could look over to where the scrip office was and see gun thugs killing men identified as being part of the union. She said she had seen many, many men shot down on the porch where they'd walk up to the window to draw out their scrip for the day. As the situation got worse, our family came back to Tennessee. My father was a strong union man. He came back to work in the mines here and to help organize the union where he'd lived and worked most of his life.

When we left Harlan County around 1931, we moved onto a mountain called Pine Mountain. The ridge we lived on was called Johnny Ridge. We lived there until I was about nine years old, when we moved back to Guy Hollow. The time we lived on Johnny Ridge was one of the happiest times I ever had in my life, because we had a really good time going to school. We walked down a mountain about three miles to school and back up every day, but we enjoyed it, because there were several kids walking along that road. We had such a good time and learned to love each other and care about what happens to people.

Not only did we learn to share with the neighbors, but our house was open. Both my grandmothers died before my parents were five years old. My mother and daddy realized what it was like not to have a real home and the family they needed to grow up with. They felt that any child without a parent was welcome at our house. My mother's father married again late in life and had some young children. When he died and left them, we raised those children, along with the twins and my younger sister, Minnie. My daddy's sister died and left a group of children, and those children stayed at our house. Ina Kemplen was a first cousin who was reared in our house; she was the daughter of my mother's sister.

Tilda as a child (left) with her older brother and sister, twins Thomas and Alene Guy, and her young cousin, Ina Kemplen

The home of Tilda's Aunt Minnie in 1926. It is typical of the houses at that time, including the one where Tilda was born.

We were never just our family. We shared everything we had with somebody. Any child or other person without a home found one at our house. When our table was spread, whatever we had to eat was for anybody who came along. My parents were the kind of people who believed that if there were sick people in the community, you went to see about them, take care of them, bring them food. If we killed a hog, we kids had to carry a mess of meat to a lot of people. A lot of times we didn't have much left when we got through taking food to the neighbors, but we learned to share everything we ever had.

So we learned to share our beds, share our food, share everything we ever had with other people. I am really proud of that, because as I've grown up and had children of my own, I've been able to help a lot of people. I keep thinking back to those times when I learned as a way of life that you didn't serve God by serving yourself. You served God by serving others. We grew up to understand that people sharing with people was the way that people got to know one another and to understand and appreciate each other.

My life was woven around that simple, humble beginning in that log cabin. Each time I start thinking back to my childhood, there's a great feeling about what I learned from my parents and what I owe them. Neither of them had education as far as going to school, but they had the greatest education in the world as to what it means to earn a living on a farm and in the coal mines and how to survive. We always had food on our table when a lot of people didn't, because while my daddy worked in the coal mines, we all worked at home and raised our own food in the gardens. We picked berries, canned apples, and did everything else that we could to make a living.

We never had much in the way of material things. But with the simple life we lived, we didn't need much. We lived a life that was good, clean, and honest. My parents guided us from childhood to adulthood with strong, loving hands and a set of standards to live by. They taught us right from wrong, and if we didn't do right, we were corrected. We were taught to believe that we were just as good as anybody else as long as we did as well as they did. I grew up with the idea that even though others might look better, nobody was better than I was. I feel that my roots were well grounded and that I had a good beginning.

I have not forgotten where I came from. I am proud to say that all I am and all I ever will be, all I do and all I ever will do I owe to my parents, who gave me a start in life through their simple way of life and their great respect for people. They had great faith in God, and they served and worshiped Him through serving others. Everything I know now and everything I've done throughout my lifetime to get to where I am with my work and my life I learned from my parents back there in those early years.

I could read and write before I ever entered public school, and I could say my ABC's backward and forward. We didn't have a lot of books, but my brother and sister had a reader. I would read along with them at night when they studied. I also read off the salt boxes and the newspapers used as wallpaper on our walls. I was reading and working with whatever was around that had printed words on it. I was born under the sign of Aries and have learned by reading my horoscope that it really fits my personality. I guess Aries children are very active and inquisitive; they're always wanting to learn. I feel that I had a good start in learning by being an Aries child, and I guess I drove my parents crazy asking questions and learning the things they knew.

I was really way ahead when I went to school. In the first grade I could read and do lots of things that some of the other kids couldn't; I guess they weren't as hyper as I was. I was so proud that I could read. I entered Primroy Elementary School in 1931 at the age of six years, along with forty-five or fifty other boys and girls. It was a one-room school with only one teacher.

You had so many people to learn from in that school that you just couldn't keep from learning if you listened. You learned what you were supposed to in your books, but you were also hearing all the other kids recite their lessons, so you couldn't help but pick up on that. Every child had the opportunity to learn everything being taught to every other child. I think the one-room school was the greatest learning institution that has ever been on this earth.

What a wonderful time we had there. Some of the fondest memories I have of my first three years of school have to do with going out under the giant oak trees to play and eat our lunch together. We carried our drinking water from a nearby spring in a water bucket and dipped it with a long-handled dipper. Each one either had a cup or made one from paper, if they had the paper. Some of the games we played were stickball, Annie Over, and Red Rover.

When school started in August, there was always a two-week revival at the little church that was close to the school. They would have church service each morning at eleven o'clock and each evening at seven. Most of our parents were at the services. The schoolteacher would line us up, and we would walk down to the morning church service. This had a great impact on the community. Our parents helped to get in coal and wood for winter. If by chance we ran out, the older boys and girls would help to find wood to keep a fire.

The biggest thrill I had in first grade was when our teacher took us one by one on his lap to teach us to tell time with his pocket watch. Another thing I remember is that when I was in third grade the teacher asked me to help the first graders read. That was my first teaching experience—helping the ABC class (that's what we had in our first year). I could help them learn to read in the first reader because I could read so well.

If we didn't do what was right, we got in trouble, at school or at home. My dad and mommy used a switch, but at school they used a paddle. There were some kids who got spankings almost every day because they'd just do mean things. There were so many of us that it was really easy to do mean things, like reach over and pinch somebody or pull hair. The room was so full of children that the teacher didn't know if someone left, either through the door or the window. If you got caught you were in trouble. But you could behave in that classroom. I never got a spanking. I always wanted to study and learn and not be into everything, because I never wanted to go home and say I'd gotten a spanking. I always had a fear of that.

After I finished third grade at the Primroy school, my family moved back to Guy Hollow, where I finished grade school in another one-room school called King School because so many people in the area were "King" by name. I went through the eighth grade. Reading and math were always favorite subjects of mine. I liked spelling, too, because it was a challenge. You had to really study for spelling. In seventh and eighth grade, I liked geography and history, because I was studying about other people and other places where I'd like to have gone.

I wanted to go to high school. All my life I wanted to be a missionary and a teacher. We lived so far back in the mountains, I couldn't go to high school. There was no transportation, and the nearest high school was twenty-five miles away. I had to walk three miles to get to a county road, which was no more than a wagon road, and then there wasn't any school bus service, even on the county road. So there was no way I could go to high school. But I never stopped wanting to go to school and learn more. I had a good eighth-grade education, though. I went through the eighth grade twice, because I wanted to go to school so badly that I repeated eighth grade to get to go another year. That is where my school years stopped until I was thirty-two years old.

In Primroy, the beautiful community where I attended the little one-room school through the third grade, there's a little white church still standing where I went from the time I was born until I was grown and married. I still go back there sometimes. That's Primroy Baptist Church, where my parents were church members. They helped build the church and supported it as long as they lived.

I grew up not knowing whether to believe everything I heard in church. I was always a little rebellious about the way the church people talked, especially the preachers. They would preach that you had to be Baptist or you went to hell. I didn't believe that. So I came up with my own set of standards and faith that I believed in, and I didn't go along with everything I heard.

The church did not satisfy me. The way the church worked when I was growing up wasn't what I believed they ought to have been doing. They weren't really helping people to live better, feel good about themselves, or have a better family life. It seemed to me that the emphasis was on going to church and trying to get to Heaven, not trying to pave ways people can follow to make a better life here on earth. Our parents taught us to be a friend to those in need, to carry their cross or burdens for them. They taught us that if a person is sick, visit them; if they are hungry, feed them; if they are sad, comfort them. I really didn't believe in the church. I didn't see it encouraging any of the things that our family believed in.

When we were growing up, we didn't know that there were any churches other than the Baptist. As I grew older, I got involved with the Methodist Church. The first experience I had with the Methodists was when the Henderson Settlement Elementary School— which is still operating in Frakes, Kentucky, in Bell County about twelve miles away—expanded to our community by building Archer Center School here. In the school was a chapel room where we had church on Sunday morning, Sunday night, and Wednesday evening, just like most churches. The Methodist Church owned the building and ran the lunch program, which the children had never had before. The county paid the schoolteachers. I really liked what I saw and what I heard. I worked in the Sunday school and on whatever there was to be done to help the community.

That was some of my first real community development work. This was more than just always being a good neighbor and doing things all my life for people. I learned a lot from the people who came as missionaries or as directors and teachers. In the early 1960s, even after I started teaching, I worked during the summers at Henderson Settlement as houseparent, cook, and Bible school teacher. I also taught second grade for half a school year. I did a lot of work with the church there and learned a lot about making my dreams become reality.

What I like about the Methodist Church is that it promotes efforts to help meet human needs. The Methodist Church did, and still does, a lot of things for people in this community and surrounding communities. It is really interested in people's welfare. I've learned a lot from church people that I've used in the programs and projects I've developed, and the church has supported our work.

The Methodist Church puts a real emphasis on the importance of getting a good education so people can live better and feel better about themselves and others. You aren't pushed to do something, but you're supported once you decide to do it. Working with church people helped me focus my attention on my own education and the need to continue with it. When I expressed my desire to further my education and become a teacher, the church helped me begin my college education.

Most people around here were Baptist. Lots of people were strict, hard-shell Baptist. They didn't like anybody else coming in with any other way of worship or way of education. My parents were older, and they understood that my involvement with the Methodist Church was good even though they had been Baptist all their lives. When I was a youngster, Henderson Settlement had a boarding school where children could go to high school. They had their own high school, like most settlement schools. There were other children from this community who went there through high school and then went on to college. My parents wouldn't let me go. They didn't know enough about it to feel comfortable sending me there. Later my high school and college education came about anyway. With faith and hope, everything I have wanted has happened.

I was married to James Kemplen when I was nineteen years old and he was twenty-seven. When my children, Ralph and Chris, were six and four years old, I got a job at Archer Center School. I was paid a small stipend to be the cook for the lunch program. Working in this school made my desire to learn and to become a teacher much stronger. I had always wanted to go back to school, and I didn't know what to do about it. I did some substitute teaching, and I ordered myself a high school course. I was going to study on my own. It wasn't impossible, but it was very hard to do with two small children and a home and a job.

One of the teachers asked me why I didn't go to college instead; I didn't know that I could. She told me there was a program in Claiborne County, Tennessee, for adults over twenty-one who wanted to go to school, even if they hadn't been to high school. The Methodist Church helped me get a scholarship, and on my thirty-second birthday, March 23, 1957, I entered this special program at Lincoln Memorial University (LMU) in Harrogate, Tennessee, for adults who hadn't finished high school. LMU accepted me even without a high school diploma provided I wanted to study and could make the grade. The courses I took the first semester were art and music on Saturdays, because that's what was being offered. I made an A and a B, so I was in. I went on to get a two-year teaching certificate and made good grades.

I went to Cumberland College in Williamsburg, Kentucky, for the next three years and got a four-year teaching certificate and a bachelor of science degree in elementary education in August 1962. It took me five years to accomplish four years of course work, because I worked all the time. My dream had become a reality so far, because I had gotten to be a teacher and would be teaching in one- and two-room schools in the coal camps and different areas.

Before I ever started to go to school to become a teacher, I talked it over with my husband, Jim, who was working a small truck mine at the time. We agreed that once I started, I wouldn't quit. I said: "We need to realize that it's going to be hard, because I'm going to

Tilda's Cumberland College
graduation picture, 1962

Tilda's students (from left) David Leach, Bill Siler, and Gary Leach,
in front of the one-room schoolhouse at Primroy (Jack Corn)

be gone. I've got to go to school, and I've got to do a lot of things I've not done before." We agreed that was all right, and he was supportive of it. Jim did what he could by helping to keep things together at home.

I know some other women who went to school at the same time I did, and their husbands were supportive of them. The women I know who tried to go to school didn't have husbands saying, "You can't" or anything. I know with us it was for a better way of life for our whole family. The big mines had closed down, and everything was pretty well phased out. It was a good opportunity to get a job.

I received no scholarship when I went to Cumberland College, so I had to do it all on my own. Both Cumberland and LMU were in sort of extreme places to have to travel to from here. I had to do a lot of traveling. I didn't drive a car, and I had to ride with somebody else. I wasn't making much money. I was still cooking at the school and made $100 a month at that time. To pay college tuition out of that was pretty rough. I never had enough money when I'd have to register for school, so I'd always have to wait until I got paid to pay on my tuition. I got a student loan from the bank. I did a little bit of everything to pay my tuition. After I got out of college, it took me ten years to pay back my loans.

It was a real struggle to go to school. I had to face all kinds of hardships, but all of it was worthwhile. It was hard working a job, keeping a home together, and having two kids to send to school and help with their lessons—along with studying my own. But it wasn't something that was impossible. I think anybody who wanted to get up and do what I did, regardless of what it took, could have done it, too. That's one of the things I've been able to do. I've set an example for local women to follow, especially the women I work with. This is what I did, and if I could do it, under the stress of having children, not driving, and all this, anybody who has the ambition can do it.

I wanted to teach because of my own love for learning. I always wanted to learn everything I could. I wanted to transfer the things

I learned to somebody else so I could help them learn. The teachers gave us a good beginning of wanting to help others learn when, way back in the third grade, they asked those who were able to read well to teach the other children. When I became a teacher, it wasn't that I wanted to do it for the money, even though I wanted to get paid and am proud I got paid. I only made $185 a month when I started teaching. I think a good teacher deserves more money than they will ever get. Sometimes I see people whose goal seems to be the money, but it certainly wasn't mine. My goal was to help the children. I don't know what else motivated me except the love for learning and for books that I've had since my own childhood. That must have been it.

I had to go out of this community to teach. I struggled through school to get an education, but because of the politics, it was hard to get a job here in Campbell County, Tennessee, where I was born and raised and where I lived. If school board members' nieces, nephews, uncles, aunts, or cousins wanted jobs, they were the ones who got them. I taught in Bell County, Kentucky, for six years before I ever got a job in Tennessee. Four years of it, I had to travel to Fonde, Kentucky, which is about six or eight miles up the road here. Two years of it was way over near Middlesboro, on what they call Upper Laurel Fork, way back out in the mountains in a two-room school. It was far. During the whole time I taught in Kentucky, I had to get a ride with anyone I could catch a ride with. It wasn't until I began teaching in Tennessee that I bought an old Volkswagen and learned to drive so I could take myself to work.

When my children attended Archer Center School, I was working as a cook there. When I got my first teaching job at Fonde Elementary School in Kentucky, I took the children with me to attend the same school; they were in different grades from those I taught. When I was transferred to Upper Laurel Fork Elementary School, my children were ready for high school. They went to Henderson Settlement High School, and I traveled on across the mountain to

Upper Laurel Fork. The main reason I brought my children with me was that I wanted to be close to the children, take part in their school activities, and keep close ties with the school they attended. I also wanted to be there when they left home and when they returned.

Fonde Elementary was a four-teacher school in the coal camp at Fonde, Kentucky. I started out teaching there in 1959, after I had gone two years to college and received a two-year temporary teaching certificate. The school was in a coal mining community where, during the days of big coal and big mining, there were nice churches, a company store, a nice stone school building, and lots of company houses. The deep mining had closed down when I taught there, but most of the houses were still left and lots of the people were still there.

One sad thing that happened while I was teaching there was that as a family left the area, the coal company sometimes tore down the house or sold it. The company no longer wanted to be liable for the houses, so they took down a lot of them and sold them to people who would move the houses to their own land and live in them or rent them out to someone else. There were not enough places for people to live.

The number of students in the school began to dwindle. In the peak of the deep mining days, the Fonde school was an eight-room school. By the time I taught there, the school had only four rooms, with one teacher for each room. I had the first and second grades the first two years I taught there.

During that time many people began to go away to find jobs. They would go north to find jobs, then have to come back because mining was the only skill they had. It was hard for them to make it in the towns, where they had to learn new skills. Most people wouldn't go and leave their families behind. They'd go get jobs and come back and get their families, so that took the kids out of school. When they couldn't make it there, that brought the children back to school. When they would come back, maybe after spending a half a year somewhere, they would be behind. The children said that the schools in the North were so different from ours. They had a really hard time achieving in school. It was a difficult time for them. It was a hard time for me, too, because I could see how frustrated they were.

Even so, I enjoyed teaching there in Kentucky, because it was my first experience teaching in a public school. I didn't know if it was better or worse than anywhere else, because I didn't know about anywhere else. The parents were great about supporting what I was trying to do for the children. They would come out and help hold any kind of activity we wanted to have, like plays or ball games.

After I taught at Fonde for two years, I went to Upper Laurel Fork for two years and then came back to Fonde for two years. Both schools were in the same county; I just got moved around. When I went to Upper Laurel Fork, it was a two-room school, so there were just two teachers for eight grades; I had the first, second, third, and fourth grades. When I came back to Fonde, I had third and fourth grades.

During the War on Poverty days, a program was initiated under a Title I grant to hire special teachers and teacher aides to lessen the classroom load on the regular teachers and to help children who were having a hard time in school. I had a teacher aide at Fonde the last year I taught there. I'd been trying all these years to get a teaching position in Campbell County. I finally did. When they started hiring the Title I teachers, that's when I got a job at the Finis Ewing Elementary School in the Tackett Creek community, where you can see the old school building with the roof all fallen in. I taught grades one through four there for one year.

In 1967 I was given the opportunity to return to the one-room school in Primroy where I'd attended first, second, and third grade. The school went from grade one through grade eight. Many of the people had moved away from the community when the coal mines closed down, and there were very few people with children left.

There were only eleven children coming to school when I taught there. A lot of schools in the old coal camps were in the same way, with out-migration and in-migration all the time. It was turmoil for the kids. They didn't have much stability in their lives, which is so important.

The year I taught in Primroy was the best year of my teaching career. When I went back there, it was almost like walking on holy ground, it was so sacred to me. That little building was a place I had learned to love so much. For me it was like going home; it was homecoming all year long. I had these beautiful children who were just like I had been; they were there and eager to learn. We had a coal stove and a water bucket to carry water in. That year we were able to get milk and different things that the children had never had before for their lunches.

When the sun was out and it was fair weather, we'd go outside and play and even study outside. It was like an open school; it was an open classroom. We would hear acorns falling off the giant spreading oak trees that were all around the schoolhouse. The atmosphere at that little school was so beautiful, sitting out under those big trees with a big playground all around. We'd hear the wind blowing. Now and then we'd hear a rooster crowing somewhere out in the community, and once in a while a car would go by. There was nothing to distract me from my teaching or to distract the children from their learning. The schoolhouse is not there any longer, but the trees are.

The greatest thing about teaching there was that four children and I walked three miles from my house to school and three miles back every day. We not only learned what we learned at school, but we learned everything from here to there. We saw the beauty of the fall, with leaves of every color falling all around. And the winter: snow and ice waterfalls, spruce and pine trees with boughs bent low. And the spring: trees budding; blossoming wildflowers waking from a long winter's sleep; all the wild animals, baby birds, blue jays, cardinals, bobwhites, squirrels, rabbits, and butterflies; everything that you would see in the great high rocks and giant trees and crossing the streams—fish, tadpoles, and frogs. It was a beautiful year for me.

We didn't have any more equipment than when I went to school there, except a table, but our seats were better. Back in the old days, I remember there were two or three children sitting in one seat. The main difference was that we had more books and more paper and pencils than we had when I went to school. Back then the parents had to buy the books. If I was in fifth grade or whatever, my dad might buy the reader, and someone else's dad would buy the speller. The families of each student would try to get one book so the whole class would have one set of books to share. I guess today if a class had just one set of books, they'd be panicking and saying they didn't have anything to learn from.

Four children out of eleven never missed a day all year. The only place they had to go was school, and they really liked going. One said proudly, "This is the first year I've ever finished a whole year of school." Some who hadn't gone to school much before put in a full year. Two of the older children who were in seventh and eighth grade were able to go on to high school the next year, because we worked hard on getting them ready. One of them graduated; I don't think the other one did.

I started another school year in Primroy with eleven children when, for some reason, the county decided to close that school. They said it was because two children weren't old enough, according to the rules and regulations. Those same two children who weren't old enough to go to school in Primroy continued to attend school at Jellico Elementary School. I always thought they closed it for some other reason, but I never really knew what it was. I was left without a job, even though I had a degree and had all this experience behind me. They thought they could close that school and not give me a job anywhere else.

I had to fight the Campbell County School Board to get another job. They had hired people who didn't even have any college work to teach school, or maybe had as little as one year. That's the kind of political thing that was going on. I went to the Tennessee Department of Education and talked with them about it. They said: "You've got your rights. If they don't hire you, they can pay you; you can sit home and draw your pay." So when I went to the county school board meeting, that's what I told the school board. I said, "I know what my rights are. I've already called the Department of Education. You can hire me or you can pay me." A school board member called me the next morning. He said they had placed me.

That's when I was placed in a Title I position at Wynn Habersham Elementary School in the community of Habersham in Campbell County. The room I was given to teach in was a dressing room off the gym. I had twelve students. Some were older students who weren't achieving in other classrooms and were having trouble. Some hadn't learned to read and write and had probably been held back for years. I got some small children, too, who were really handicapped; several had cerebral palsy. Some were hyperactive. I was trying to teach twelve children there in that dressing room with ball games going on and all the distractions that go on in a gym. These children were easily distracted anyway.

It was an almost impossible situation. There wasn't much I could do for them. My room was overcrowded with children who had nothing in common; there was no common thread to catch on to. It was a dumping ground; I was the only one there to get them. Title I was supposed to alleviate the overcrowding of classrooms and provide children with special help. But what happened to me was that I got too many who needed special help; it was just sort of doled out to me.

Then one day my supervisor came out and was standing in the door talking to me. As she was leaving, one of the little boys whizzed a pencil at her, right by her head. Of course, it kind of scared her.

I said to her: "Is there anything we can do about setting up some special education program here so that we can have a better situation? Maybe I'll be able to help these children."

She could see what was going on, and she said: "There is a training program we can pay for if you're willing to go. In one summer you can get your endorsement in special education, and you can set up a special education classroom. Are you willing to go and retrain?"

I said, "I sure am."

In 1970 I went to the Tennessee Technological University in Cookeville for two four-hour courses. I earned eight credits in two weeks. We went to school about eight hours a day to get those four credits in each course. From there I went to the University of Tennessee and spent the rest of the summer getting my endorsement certificate in special education.

I came back to Wynn Habersham School that fall and was able to set up a special education class, get the kids tested and screened, get supplies and materials to work with, and get a trailer to work out of. It was a big thing to get those kids into a situation where they could be treated and taught the way they needed to be. We wouldn't have just any child who was maybe overage in the class, but there would be a good possibility of helping the children achieve according to their abilities. That was the only special education program for grades kindergarten through twelve that served the whole area. Jellico and the town schools already had special education, but that little mountain school didn't have it. So that was one of my great achievements.

I moved on from special education to teaching fourth grade one year, because the school needed a fourth grade teacher. I enjoyed that, because I had a lot of brilliant students. I also had a lot who weren't so well off in school, but some of the brightest children I've ever taught were in that fourth grade class. A lot of them have gone on to college and done really well.

At first, when special education was in the trailer, the children from other classrooms would call it "the crazy trailer." I don't know if they made it up or where they heard that. Of course, children are smart; they can put it together. They would shy away and wonder what was going on back there, because it was behind the school building. But I did a lot of arts and crafts with the children and let them do things that brought out their talents and their beauty; the other children would see that. The librarian was my good friend, and I asked her if we could put some of their things in the library so others could see them. Then everyone could see that the special education children were doing prettier things and learning things that the others weren't able to participate in. After that, some of the other children came in during recess time to do arts and crafts with us.

I really enjoyed helping children in a special way. I wanted them to be tested so I could work with them on their grade level. But when the testing was done, they were labeled "mentally retarded." That was very disturbing. The school had what they called cumulative folders, and each teacher was supposed to rate the children at the end of the school year. I was supposed to tell the teacher who got them the following year what each child's attitude was and what their academic skills were. I refused to do much in those folders. When I got a child in my classroom, I was supposed to go back and get his or her folder and look at it. I didn't want to look at it, because I wanted to take the children where I found them and not look at what some other teacher had said about them.

My philosophy about teaching was that you take children wherever you find them. You don't listen to anything anyone else says about how they'd done and how they'd acted the year before. You just take them and learn for yourself what they can do and work on their level. They achieve much more that way than if you try to go by a curriculum where they have no comprehension of what you're talking about. So I had a rebellious thing going on there with education in general, and the labeling of children was something I could hardly stand.

Seeing the special education children labeled "mentally retarded" when they were only environmentally deprived made me feel that I was fighting a losing battle. I was helping those children in a way, but in another way they were still labeled, probably for life. So I began to think about what could be done to help the children. It came to me that preschool education was the answer. I had the realization that we needed to start teaching children at an earlier age. Feed them, love them, play with them, teach them skills before they ever enter the school system.

I had a real conviction that if we could have started prenatally, if the mothers had had better care and better nutrition and had known how to get health care and prenatal care, the children would have been better off. And I remembered back to my own preschool days and how much I had learned before I entered school. I'd learned a lot of things that helped me, like reading, writing, spelling, counting— everything that had meant something to me. I realized that children needed a good beginning in skills training, and they needed to have good nutrition and care that maybe a family with lots of children in the home couldn't give. It kept coming back to me: this is what children need. I began to talk about it to parents and to teachers.

Of course, some of the teachers thought I was crazy. They told me, "I don't know why you would even think of doing something that you're not getting paid for."

I said: "Well, I'm going to do it. Just watch me. I'm going to keep on being crazy, if that's what it takes to get something done."

As I talked about it to parents or anyone I could come into contact with, I found that many people were very disturbed about their children failing in the first few years of school. After children had failed several times in their early years, nothing was going forward; it was all going backward. So by the time they reached fifth or sixth grade, they were dropping out of school. If children can't achieve by the teachers' standards and the standards set up by the people who make up the national achievement testing materials, they can't go forward. When children begin to go backward and can't achieve, they're put back in lower grades. Where else can they go but home? Children don't want to go to school when they know that they're going to go in the wrong direction, or that people are going to send them in the wrong direction.

The principal of Jellico High School gave me some statistics he uses about our area. He said that for every two children who start first grade, one of them finishes high school; so there's a 50 percent dropout rate. One of the reasons the dropout rate is so high is that the children from back in the mountains have to come out from there to go to high school in Jellico; they're on buses a long time, morning and evening. Another reason is the children who have to go to schools outside their own area tend to feel intimidated by the teachers and the other children. I know that children still say they don't fit in at Jellico High School. Somehow in a town, the doctors' and lawyers' children seem to think they're a little better than children who come from way back here in the mountains and don't have as much as they do.

When my own children went to Jellico High School, one incident happened when my daughter, Chris, and her girlfriend, a neighbor, went to a ball game at the school. A girls ball team came into the dressing room where they had left their clothes and other belongings, and someone had stolen money out of their pockets. Because Chris and her girlfriend had gone to the bathroom, they got accused. Chris said she just stood up and told them: "My Mama always taught me that what I had was all I needed, that I didn't have to take anything that belonged to anyone else. We didn't take the money, and you had better be trying to find out who did." When they found out, it was one of the town doctors' daughters. My children said that was typical of how they were treated.

A lot of things have been done over the past few years to try to help children who were getting behind in school. All over the United States, the facts and figures have shown that for all of the billions of dollars that have been poured into the schools—for Title I teachers, special education teachers, teacher aides, music teachers, art teachers, and everything else that has been tried since the poverty programs started—the children were no better off than they were if they hadn't had any of this. If we had continued with the one-room schools, with teachers teaching children and not subjects, without all the frills of the programs, the children would have been able to learn and achieve more and been basically better off.

I always had an open classroom. I tried to teach children, not subjects. One young man told me about how his wife tried to teach that same way but found it very hard in this area. The school systems are sort of set up to teach between two book covers and four walls. I taught the children whatever and wherever they needed. If it meant going out in the yard to work, going out on the creek bank and letting them fish, that's what I did.

I believe that if you can capture children's interest, you can help them. If you don't, they may sit through classrooms for five, six, or eight years and not achieve too much, because you're not teaching on their level. You're not doing what they need. Book learning is not all that children want; they need experiences. I feel that children have a right to what they need instead of us imposing something on them that maybe they're not interested in.

I care a lot about the people I've taught with, and I don't mean to put them down. But most of the time teachers come to school all dressed up with nice clothes and hairdos. They stand out and stand over children. Children who are not dressed so well might feel badly about it. I've seen teachers who couldn't have gotten out and played with children, because they had on high-heeled shoes and really nice clothes. I never had nice clothes and never wanted them. I still don't want them; I just want plain, simple clothes. I've always wanted to wear what I could work in, not what I could sit behind a desk in.

When I taught at Wynn Habersham and the other places I taught, I worked with the children on their level. I managed to find resources to meet their needs. I wouldn't put children down because they were sick or their heads were hurting. Instead of giving them an aspirin, I'd try to find out if they'd had anything to eat. If children were hungry, I got them a box of milk or anything else they needed so they could work better. If they needed clothes, I went and found them. If they needed a pencil and paper, I could always pull them out of my desk. If they were unhappy, I was their friend. I didn't worry too much about the books, to tell the truth about it. The children did learn. I did some things with books, because they needed that. Mainly I tried to teach self-confidence and self-esteem.

Those children who had problems and had gotten behind in school needed special help. The school wanted us to use old textbooks for the same children who couldn't achieve in those textbooks the year before. I wouldn't go along with that; I got special material for my children to work with. Some of the Laubach method reading books I'm using now in adult education are what I taught my schoolchildren with. Being a teacher for sixteen years in the public classroom, I learned a lot from the children, and I learned a lot of the ways that children learn.

Many of the hundreds of children I had the opportunity to teach and who influenced my life have finished high school and gone to college. Many own their own businesses or hold good jobs. A young man who was in my special education class now owns his own restaurant. One girl I taught in fourth grade has now finished college and is working with the Tennessee Department of Human Services, working closely with our organization on children's issues.

Many young people had no choice but to leave the area to find employment. They come home every chance they get. I did everything I could to motivate them to be successful wherever they went, in whatever they attempted to do. I wanted to help them develop a sense of self-worth and self-motivation so they would feel proud of themselves and be in control of their own lives, as much as the economic conditions of the area and the political systems would allow. Lots of my former students who now have children of their own still call me "Mom."

When I was growing up, I looked at teachers as being very special people, which they are. After I was grown and became a mother, I realized that my parents were the best teachers I'd ever had. It was that teaching that probably helped me to believe and think the way I do. I knew that I was with my children more than any teacher would ever be, and I had to be a teacher to them. When I became a public schoolteacher, which had been my hope, dream, and goal all my life, I also felt very strongly that I needed to teach children. Although parents are their first and best teachers, I hoped to contribute to their learning in a way that would give them a solid foundation to grow on.

I believe that we're all teachers. I realized during the time I taught that parents thought the teacher ought to be able to do anything. I tried to help them realize that I was just like them. I was not only a teacher; I was a mother, and I was just a normal, local person. I had been to school, but they knew more about many things than I did. We're all teachers. Teachers do all they can in a classroom, but the real teaching has to go beyond the classroom.

I love to teach. There's glory in it. No matter how hard the struggle, I will not quit. For each child is precious, regardless of who they are or where they come from. They are children today, doctors, lawyers, preachers, teachers, and the parents of children tomorrow. I hope that my involvement with children has made the path softer, safer, and brighter as they travel the long way toward adulthood. I hope I have been able to scatter a few rose petals along the way and make each life a bit happier and a speck brighter. Children have made my life worthwhile and given me a dream to follow, from "my humble roots to beautiful roses."

Two

My Work

COMMUNITIES IN NEED

I'd like to give some history of the Central Appalachian region, including my home area, the Clear Fork Valley, in the mountains of East Tennessee bordered by Cumberland Mountain and Pine Mountain. During the early days of our country, people came from all parts of the world for one reason or another: freedom, religion, wealth. People who penetrated these mountain ranges of Appalachia found them to be rich in animal life, timber, coal, and iron ore. When word reached England about the rich coal and iron ore beds in these mountains, men were sent to buy up this land from the people who knew little of its worth. The American Association, a British landholding company, thought that the iron ore found in the Cumberland Gap section, across the mountain from where I live, would give rise to another Pittsburgh steel city. But they didn't find so much iron ore as coal, soon to be known as King Coal. With this company owning the land and leasing it to coal companies, mines could be opened anywhere they found enough coal.

Before the days of the buying up of the land and the beginning of coal mining, everyone owned their land and farmed it to earn their living. With the opening of the mines and the opportunity for men to get jobs digging coal with a pick and loading it with a shovel, many families sold their land to the landholding companies and moved into coal company houses in company towns. In these coal camps, they shopped at company stores, attended company churches, and went to company doctors. They were never free of company demands. As the song goes, "They owed their souls to the company store." Scrip was money issued by a particular coal company as payment to miners in the coal camps. It could be used only at the company store. If a man lived outside the company camps, he wasn't much thought of by company officials. Some men walked as many as ten miles to work and ten miles back home. They would trade their day's earnings and carry it home on their backs.

During the early years of my growing up, my father worked in the mines when there was work, but many times the mines would be closed because no orders came for their coal. Other times there were wildcat strikes, where men walked off their jobs because of ill treatment by the companies. Then there would be picket lines to keep the companies from giving their jobs to anyone who would take them. Many men were killed while defending their right to work and be treated fairly. The women and children had to live with the fear of their fathers, husbands, and sweethearts being killed during the strikes or while they were miles underground in the worst working conditions imaginable. I always lived with these fears; both my father and my husband were coal miners.

In the 1930s and 1940s union organization came to try to protect working men's rights. With this came more strikes, fighting, murder, and much unrest in the coal mining areas. After many years of hard work and struggle, the United Mine Workers of America became a way for miners to gain better working conditions and better wages. Then in the late 1940s, the companies brought machinery to the underground coal mines. One machine could do the work of many men, so jobs became harder to get and to keep. During the late 1940s and early 1950s, surface mining became the industry of the area, providing very few jobs and no community services. But it destroyed our once-beautiful mountains and streams. Surface mining, also called strip mining, was seen as a cheaper and easier way to get the coal out. This kind of mining also used fewer people. It was mainly operated by a person who might be able to get hold of a piece of machinery and lease a piece of land and go to work on it. As surface mining grew bigger and more of it was being done, the companies grew from one-man operations to firms with several men working. So there were some jobs, but strip mining never provided enough jobs. It usually was the operator's family or friends who worked at those jobs.

As with deep mining, even though some of the people who operated surface mining were local people, all the wealth was taken out and nothing was put back into the area in the way of roads, schools, medical services, housing, or anything else. Surface mining was not a source of salvation for the people. People had learned enough about where the coal was, and it was an easy way to get it out. But it was very destructive to a lot of the land. The surface mining often came in too close to people's homes and made lakes and dams that were dangerous and did a lot of damage. Flooding caused destruction to land and houses, as well as some deaths.

Strip mining also brought violence with it. There were people, both miners and others, who didn't like the idea of strip mining, because it was destroying the mountains and houses and anything in the way. People who had been involved in deep mining were furious at strip mining coming in because of the destruction taking place. In addition, they thought that the reason they lost their jobs was stripping coming in. There was a terrible struggle between strip miners and those who objected to it. Machinery was destroyed, and lives on both sides were endangered. Many men lost their lives during this period of unrest.

When the jobs in company mines went, so did the housing, the stores, the doctors—everything and everybody people had depended on for years. People didn't have anything to depend on for income and for housing and a way of life. They lost everything. Almost everyone had to go somewhere else to find jobs. All during the 1950s, many men went away to work in the industrial cities in northern and midwestern states, including Ohio, Michigan, and Indiana. Some tried to stay here. Even during the hard times, my family didn't leave the area; we stayed here. But there were so many people who were out of work immediately that it was really hard.

The men didn't know which way to turn. When the larger deep mines closed, my husband, Jim, and his brother, along with all the other men who didn't leave the area, opened small truck mines wherever there was some coal and tried to make a living that way. It was still deep mining underground, but it was small, not like one of the company mines. This was a very hard and dangerous mining operation, with no safety measures at all. The union men who were not working the truck mines began trying to close down the operations by picketing the men who were trying to make a living and who also were union men. It was just that their operations couldn't qualify for United Mine Workers of America membership, because they were too small.

The worst thing I saw happening to families was the going and coming. Many people went on to the cities, but a lot of them didn't make it because they didn't have any skills besides mining, and a lot of them didn't have much education to learn another skill or to cope with city life. They would come back home without a place to live. Many of the houses that existed in the coal camps were left empty as people moved away to find work. As the company houses became unoccupied, the coal company sold them to somebody to tear down and build a house of their own, or else somebody would burn them down. It became a very frightening experience for people, because if they went away to work and came back, they wouldn't have anywhere to live. Then they'd have to move in with family. One family just didn't have enough space for another family to move in.

We live in an area where there are few jobs and fewer houses owned by families who occupy them. During the past twenty years of operating a child care center and many other programs, we have experienced the problem of many parents and children who didn't know from morning to evening what they could call home. People don't have jobs to pay the rent even if they could find a house. They may pay it for one month and find they can't pay it a second month, and they have to move out. They might move out and go to Kentucky or somewhere one month, and they may be back living in the same place the next month. The children have to go to school wherever their parents happen to be.

Many have been forced to move to towns where federally subsidized housing is available, thus causing marital problems and the uprooting of family ties. When young families have to go out of their communities to the towns to get subsidized housing, lots of times that doesn't work out. They're used to living out in the communities, maybe not really close to each other, and then they're put into apartments where there are lots of other people and other families. We've seen couples get divorced.

When people don't have jobs and can't make any money to have their own houses, when they have to go on welfare and food stamps and live in houses owned by some landlord somewhere just because the rent is lower, they are not in charge of anything in their lives. Somebody else is in charge of everything they get and everything they do. When you take away their responsibility, you take away their pride, because if they have nothing to say about what their houses are like or about how much money they earn, if they can't get any more food stamps than what you'll give them, then they have no control. When people have no control of what's going on in their lives, they can't be very happy, and they can't have a stable life.

In this kind of situation, people become very frustrated and upset, and they lose hope and faith in most everything. When people can't survive and help their families to make it, they feel helpless and hopeless. A lot of times the people I work with don't have faith or hope because they don't really have anything to encourage them to be better off or to do the things that they need to do. Without education and a job and a home where they can anchor their roots and raise their children, anyone would lose hope. Sometimes I've seen people with such a hopeless look in their eyes, especially the men who always worked in the mines so they could feed their families and take care of them. I've felt very helpless at times, but I've never had that hopeless feeling.

Back during the time when everybody was out of work and husbands were leaving home to go north to find jobs, sometimes they took their families along and sometimes they didn't, according to whether they could get a good enough job to take care of a family there. They couldn't take care of a family here and themselves there; it was really hard for the whole family. When I was growing up, the father was usually the person who disciplined the children. With the father out of the home, it became very hard for the mother to hold the home together, discipline the children, and take care of everything. I saw lots of homes that were really torn apart by separations; sometimes divorce came into it.

I don't know how much mental abuse might have gone on, screaming and scolding. That can very easily happen when people are disturbed about not having a job or a house or disturbed about not being able to go to the doctor when they need to. Lots of people couldn't go to the doctor when they needed to, and they'd get all nervous and upset. Alcohol was a problem. When men couldn't work, it was easy to turn to alcohol. When you're frustrated and you don't know which way to turn, it's easy to turn to something that puts a mask over your face or blinds you to the situation. There's still a lot of alcohol used, and in the last few years, drugs have become a very big problem in the area.

It's been a real struggle for both men and women in the last twenty years. It's been easier for a woman than for a man to get work sewing at home or get a job with a sewing factory. I do know a lot of men who have gone to the shirt factories and the other sewing factories to work, because they need men to do certain things. Part of the struggle is that men still hope that coal is going to come back and really be a strong industry. But I don't see that, because there are too many other types of power plants. Coal is not king any longer. The price of coal hit bottom. It's not used as much as it used to be, and it's been stripped away here so there's not enough coal for the industry to be like it once was. There may be plenty of coal, there may be mountains of it that have not been touched, but what's been easy to get has been gotten.

There are very few jobs left. Lots of people had jobs driving coal trucks while surface mining was going on. If they could get coal trucks, they could lease on with a company. Then they had their own jobs. But up and down the roads now you can see lots of coal trucks sitting empty, not being used. Up until the mid-1980s, the coal trucks were running every day, but now you'll seldom see them running even one day a week. Those kinds of jobs are gone.

When I'm talking about the need for jobs, I have people ask me why people don't leave. My answer is, "Where would they go?" They don't have anywhere else to go. I understand that in the northern towns where most people went to work, there's not a lot of work either. You hear every day on the news that plants and factories have closed down. The kind of work that many people could do is no longer there. If people don't have the skills and the education to get a job in Nashville, Knoxville, Oak Ridge, Ohio, or wherever else, why go? If they're not trained for the jobs, they can't make it. There's an economic crunch all over the country now. It's not easy to go from here to Chicago, Detroit, or anywhere else and get a job.

Most of the people I know choose to stay here and try to make a living, even though it may not be what they could make if they were in one of those towns. But they feel much better about themselves when they're at home and they're making whatever living they can. People have roots. They are rooted in their families. That's something that you don't break away from easily. I've not seen too many people come into our area from big cities and stay, because they're no more comfortable coming here and trying to put down roots than we are going to New York City and trying to put down roots. People who come here may stay for a while, but then they leave. We go there for a while sometimes to work and do what we have to. But every time a person gets a chance, they come back home. A lot of the men did go away to work, but if there's anything they can do back home, anything that encourages them to come back, they do.

One really big problem we had to deal with because of all the coming and going was junked cars. During the years of out-migration, when people had to go somewhere to try to find work, the number of people in the valley dropped from twelve thousand to twelve hundred. That many people were going and coming, and when they would get somewhere and get a job and earn enough to buy an old car, they would probably only have enough money to get home with it. It would break down on them, and they couldn't drive it back, so it got junked. The valley was just covered up. Every yard and every roadside had a lot of junked cars on it.

In the early 1960s, while attention was focused on the Appalachian area by government agencies and news media, community folks were realizing the need for health services, jobs, housing, education, and training beyond the mining and homemaker skills. In the days when people worked in the mines, the company took care of their needs, including housing, schools, and doctors. The people who lived out in the mountains away from the coal camps had no services. That's just the way it was. Governments were not used to having to supply services for the people of this area. The counties taxed the coal companies so little that the tax base was too small to provide services when the coal camps were closed down. People in the Clear Fork Valley area began to organize the efforts of the local community to try to help themselves and each other. This was hard but not impossible.

Under the Economic Opportunity Act of 1964, the Office of Economic Opportunity (OEO) came into being, supposedly offering a solution to the poverty-stricken areas of our nation. Many people profited by it, mainly the people who directed the programs. What I experienced with the program was that the most needy people were not the best taken care of. In fact, they were most often left out. Many other federal agencies were born around this time, including the U.S. Department of Housing and Urban Development (HUD) and the Appalachian Regional Commission (ARC). The programs and services of these agencies were supposed to relieve the pain and suffering of the "poor" people. But the poor got poorer, and the rich got richer.

Only when community-based, nonprofit organizations began to emerge did the people have any power or authority over their lives or their communities. Even then, they had to look to agencies like the ARC, the Tennessee Valley Authority (TVA), and the Commission on Religion in Appalachia (CORA). All available monies were channeled through these organizations, and it was hard for local groups to get resources directly. It was a real struggle to get help from anyone to do anything.

Attention was focused on our area when the *Nashville Tennessean* newspaper wrote a story about "the valley of despair," with pictures to show the conditions. Missionaries, university students, news people, freelance writers, and photographers flooded the area, offering their services. Many local community people were meeting, organizing around the needs, and trying to figure out where to find support for the services that were needed. The students and missionaries helped us find resources, make contact with people, and find some financial support for projects being undertaken, such as crafts cooperatives, health services, legal services, and more. They took leadership in organizing and developing. Most community people were happy about that.

I was grateful, but not happy. I realized early on that once again people were becoming as dependent upon people who came to the area as they had been on the mining companies. As we worked on projects and issues, I always raised that as a concern: we, the community people, must learn to have control of our lives and communities or else we would be faced with the same problems we had when the companies decided to move out. All the way back through the years, churches have sent people into the mountains to try to help us do things. Some of them have been very good at helping to bring resources and educational and other programs to the communities. But there's always that tension of their staying and taking ownership of everything they have helped to develop and never turning it over to the community people.

I'm very critical of people who hold power over others, and maybe the reason I am so critical is because I am a local person. I've taken on the responsibility of getting an education for myself and have encouraged others to do the same. There's some power in the community when people get a better education and have more control over their own destiny and what goes on in their community.

It becomes a struggle then, because according to some others, we're not supposed to be educated. We're not supposed to be able to organize and operate programs. We're not supposed to be intelligent or be able to make a living and be independent. That's how the outside world looks at Appalachia and its people. People are able to do anything they have the opportunity to do. As is true all over the world, some people are lazy. Some people are all the things they call us, ignorant and poor and worthless, but certainly not everyone. The majority of the people are intelligent. They may not have had an opportunity to go to school, but it doesn't mean they're not intelligent. To me, their kind of education—being educated by life experience and learning by doing for themselves—is worth much more than that of highly educated people from somewhere else who come down on people and make them feel intimidated and unworthy.

I've never approved of anyone coming into a community with

his own agenda and working for the people, not with the people. Through working with various churches and organizations over the years, I've experienced that many come to our communities with an agenda and a preconceived idea of what needs to be done for people. Some have been very helpful and are really appreciated by most of the community folks. I try to let them all know how I feel. I believe that to build a lasting relationship with people anywhere, you have to try to build a partnership with the people of the community, because they are the ones who have made the community what it is. They are also the ones who will remain there. Regardless of how much good work a church, a clinic, or any organization does in a community, the community people have to be involved. They must feel a sense of responsibility and ownership. Let us never take away the opportunity for people to do for themselves whenever they can, because when we do, we also take away their pride and their freedom, their self-esteem and self-respect.

The community organizing in our area began during the late 1950s and early 1960s, around the time of the unrest because of unemployment, the absence of health services, and very poor, run-down schools. There were unsafe conditions, with children sick and dying from hepatitis from water pollution caused by mining. Miners were sick and dying from mining-related diseases, with no organized service support systems. Louise Adams, a woman who was a great legend in her own time, served as postmistress in Clairfield, Tennessee, for a period of thirty-one years, through the boom and bust of deep mining. When she lost a son to hepatitis from unsafe water, she began to organize around that issue, along with other parents who had lost children from hepatitis. This was the health issue that caused the area to get some attention from the state board of education, the news media, and the county health departments. After a few years, Clairfield got a new school. About twenty-five to thirty years later, a water utility system was installed.

The men were the ones who traditionally went out to work in the mines. In the past, the women stayed home and did lots of things to help make a living. They raised the gardens, did the cooking, and canned and preserved the food. They nursed the sick and cared for the children. They were also involved with community activities. The women have always been the people who made their communities work. They have always taken care of anything that had to be done in the schools and the churches. It was natural for the women to go to meetings and get together in groups.

So when we first started trying to organize ourselves to do something to make our area a better place to live, a place where we could stay and survive, some men helped, but the women were mainly the ones who came out to the meetings. They were the ones who expressed their opinions about the problems and what needed to be done. From that grew some strong organizations whose board members were mostly women. We organized ourselves into groups that could work on special issues that were on people's minds and were closest to their hearts. We tried to deal with environmental problems, including the valley being full of junked cars.

One of the first things we tried to do as a group of people was to get some health services, because a lot of other people were sick, especially the miners who had worked in the deep mines. A lot of miners couldn't go away to work and couldn't do anything else because they were sick with black lung and other coal miners' diseases. Everyone who ever worked in the deep mines could qualify for black lung benefits, if they could ever get through the red tape to get them.

Another thing we worked on was job creation. Most of the women had learned to sew. They had quilted and made clothes all their lives. They helped the family make a living by making things that the family used. One of the first groups we organized was a crafts operation, Model Valley Folk Arts, in support of the community women who wanted to do craft items such as quilts, pillows, and handbags. Model Valley Folk Arts gave support to help establish a community organization based in Clairfield, the Model Valley Development Council, that could try to develop more jobs and work in other ways to help revitalize our area. The name *Model Valley* was adopted from the Model Cities program to represent people's determination to improve conditions in our rural communities.

I helped organize, develop, and implement several community-based, nonprofit organizations, serving on boards, helping to write proposals, and making personal contacts with agencies and churches. I soon realized that all the service areas we were working on primarily involved adults. I was interested in all the issues and needs, but one kept eating away at me: the children. Being a teacher in the rural coal camps and remote communities made me aware of the needs of the children. When things are bad, children hurt the most.

I had a dream and a vision of what needed to be done to help the children; hardly anyone believed that it could become a reality. No one wanted to listen to my dream and my ideas, except parents who had several children. They were concerned about their children failing in school and dropping out by the time they reached fifth grade. My idea of preschool education was unheard of in the area. Beginning in 1967, we organized around preschool children, from birth to six years old. There were two mothers who each had eight children; three in each family were preschool children. These two mothers and I became the group to provide child care services. We quickly learned that we had to have money to provide services. We began to write to churches and agencies, asking for their support.

Here again, this organizing wasn't easy, but it wasn't impossible. We followed our dream and looked for support from anywhere there might be a resource, regardless how small. The parents I worked with and I had faith, and we were not afraid to step out on that faith. I went on to organize and develop an organization that I have been directing for over twenty years, one that encourages people to be proud of who they are and to remember that they are important, that what they think and say is just as important as what anyone else thinks, says, or does.

THE CHILD CARE AND
DEVELOPMENT CENTER

Developing a child care center in this rural, mountainous area was very difficult in the early days. What I wanted to do and saw the greatest need for wasn't getting much attention from a lot of people. All the time I was helping with other projects in the valley, this thing about the children was really tugging at me. We were concerned about everything but them. Because I was a teacher, I wanted to help the children to be better off. I thought, no matter what we do for older people, if the children are left behind and not cared for, there won't be any future for this valley or anywhere else. Children are our greatest resource.

I talked with some of the people on the Model Valley Development Council board and with the Model Valley crafts group. I told them of my interest in a child care center to help the children. At that time, I didn't know whether there was any money anywhere for child care, but I knew it was a great need, and I was willing to try it. The groups I worked with didn't believe it could be done or didn't believe that I could do it. Anyway, they turned me down. They didn't want to be part of my board and didn't want to be part of getting it going.

They said: "You can't work with government. You can't work with the county."

When they kept telling me that I couldn't do this and I couldn't do that, I said: "Well, you just watch me. I'll just show you that I can. I'm going to do something, no matter how it turns out."

So I had to go on my own. I quit talking to people who were trying to do other things and began to talk to people who cared about the children. These were parents with four or six or eight children in the home, and they really needed child care. They were the ones concerned about what happened to the children. They wanted to see them have a better education and were willing to help make it happen. Mostly it was mothers who were experiencing the difficulty of their children failing in school and dropping out by fifth or sixth grade who were concerned about preschool education. These mothers and I began to have meetings wherever we could: at my house or their houses or out in the fields. We began to talk about what we could do, just as mothers who cared about the children.

It was hard to sell the child care concept to other parents, especially parents on welfare, who had trouble with the welfare people removing the children from the home or threatening to remove them. It was really hard for us to prove that we weren't the welfare department, that we weren't part of the welfare system that the parents had to be so careful of. It took about three years for people to feel really safe and good about us. We just kept saying: "We work with the Department of Human Services, but we don't work for them. We are not going to do anything to cause the children to be removed from the home." That was one of the real threats to parents.

Some parents even thought that if they didn't keep the child at home and take good care of it themselves, the welfare people would get on them. I don't know what made them think that, but we'd tell them: "The welfare office refers children to us. They're not going to take your child because you send it to the day care program. If you send it to day care, they feel you're doing a good job caring for it."

We still have some cases of people who are a little leery. All you hear on television about bad day care centers makes people more cautious. I don't blame them for being leery. We just tell them to come and visit for as long as they want to. They can come anytime, drop in without notice, and see for themselves what's going on.

It took a long, long time to get people in the community, as well as those working for the county and the state, to recognize what I was trying to do. It was a real struggle. People thought that even six years old was an early age to send children to school. Home is the finest place in the world for a child, but sometimes the mother needs some relief from four or five children. She needs to be trying to make a living for them. It took a long time to get the concept over to people and get them to believe that children should be away from their mothers if they needed the care we could give and if mothers had to work or go to school.

When this idea of setting up a child care center started floating around in my head, I talked about beginning with prenatal care for expectant mothers. I spoke with some of the people who were trying to set up clinics and with Bill Dow and others from the Appalachian Student Health Coalition (ASHC), the community health outreach program that is the "parent" project of the Center for Health Services at Vanderbilt University in Nashville. They said that we couldn't run a prenatal program without a doctor. We weren't able to have a doctor or a nurse in our organization to do that part of the work.

So we started with what we could do. My college degree would allow me to get something going by setting up a preschool education program. We had no money, no building, and not much interest out in the communities. I was still teaching school to support myself and the organization. Without my commitment and dedication to this ministry, it could never have become a reality. When I use the word *ministry*, I don't mean preaching; I mean service to people.

When I was a child, we had very few books. We had very few things. We had no pretty colored crayons to work with that would stimulate a child's interest. I guess I was stimulated by things outside, such as trees, flowers, nuts, berries, stones, fish, birds, and other animals. But some children just stayed home until they were six years old, and sometimes their homes didn't have books or other materials that let mothers help their children learn. A lot of mothers didn't realize that their children needed this early stimulation.

So I felt that those children were environmentally deprived of the things that normally would stimulate their interest in learning, things that children out in the cities or towns or wherever probably had. We had very few resources, but we tried to set up a program that was stimulating and beautiful for the children so they'd want to be there and want to learn. That early stimulation of interest and the love we give them are the real things children need to become better off and not be so backward that they get labeled "retarded" when they go to school.

I know from teaching first grade that when many children come to first grade, they've never been away from their mothers, and their mothers have never been away from them. The mothers have a really hard time too. They come to school and can't leave their children, who are screaming and carrying on. We feel that we've been able to help preschool children get used to being in a place other than home. They learn to adjust to other children and adults and to have relationships other than with their mothers. This helps them through a really hard time when they go to school.

I'm asked many times where the parents work. Some of them work if they can find jobs, but there are few jobs in this area, except those provided by the nonprofit organizations that have sprung up. We didn't develop child care for working parents; it was set up for children. It was organized by mothers who cared about the children, for every child who needed the services. Some of the children from Jellico have one white and one black parent. Some of the children are part Indian, because most of the people around this area have Cherokee heritage. We accept children regardless of their race, creed, or color, or what their parents do or don't do, or anything else. The criterion for getting in our center is being a child.

We made a commitment in those early years—at the very first meetings we had to start organizing ourselves—that we would never turn a child away from our door. We have never had to yet. It's been really hard to make it with limited resources, but we've never had to turn down parents who needed their children in day care. We've been overflowing with children, but we always find a way to take care of them. And we're constantly trying to build and have more space and more programs that they can be part of.

Almost every day we have thirty to forty children; sometimes we get way up to the sixty mark. They're from newborn to six years old, which is another unique thing that was unheard of, even where there were day care centers around the cities and towns, like Knoxville, Oak Ridge, and LaFollette. Everybody was going with the three-to-five-year-old programs for children who would be going to school pretty soon. They didn't want to deal with the infants and toddlers. We felt that if, for example, a mother had a three-week-old infant and a three-year-old toddler, if we took the three-year-old into the program, the mother had no better chance to get out and try to find a job or try to go to school or try to do anything else she needed to unless she could also find care for her infant.

We had a real struggle with the state's licensing department before we could serve infants. They normally say six weeks to six years. In our proposal we said newborn to six years old. We won that battle early. We didn't proceed until they agreed that we could do it, because we felt that the younger we got the children into services, the better start they would have through the care they received.

After we got the Mountain Communities Child Care and Development Centers going, we found ourselves in a position where we said, "We're going to do something for the children," but we didn't have a building or any money. So what we decided to do was to prove ourselves by having summer programs with an all-volunteer staff. We ran our first summer program in White Oak in 1968. We got the use of a shelter provided by the White Oak Church of Christ. The volunteers worked with children from tiny babies to school-age children, so we had both big and little children. That first summer, the JFG Coffee Company in Knoxville, Tennessee, gave us peanut butter and we got bread or crackers so all the children could have lunch. I don't remember how we got everything, but we got things donated. We'd buy or bring from home whatever we could.

From 1969 to 1973, we had summer programs in six different communities. We were spread over the whole rural area: White Oak, Stinking Creek, Clairfield, Morley, Roses Creek, and Primroy. We often had no place to have the summer programs, but the parents were willing to help. If somebody would let us clean up a field so we could have a place where the children could play, we could work during the summer. If it rained, it meant we had to go, but if the sun shone and it was nice out, we just had our programs out in the field. When the U.S. Department of Agriculture summer feeding program came out, we were able to get food for all the children.

It was a real beginning out there in those open fields. The summer activities brought children together with other people and helped them to develop socially. We read stories, played organized games, and helped the older children with their math and other subjects. But when summer was over, the bigger children would go back to school, and I would have to go back to school. The mothers and little children had to just go home, because there was nowhere else to go.

We never let that stop us. We kept on thinking about what we could do. We kept on meeting, plotting, and planning. We'd take trips down to Knoxville to look at ragged, old trailers we might use for a shelter. One time we found an old, single-wide trailer in Knoxville that we could pay two hundred dollars down on to take over the payments. The Model Valley Development Council that I'd helped organize and was part of at that time gave us the $200 as a donation; that was our first money.

After we got the trailer, we had a really hard time because we didn't have a place to set it. So Lou Malicoat, a longtime public school teacher, let us set it by the side of the road out in front of her house in Little White Oak. That was in 1973, the year we became a nonprofit, tax-exempt organization, Mountain Communities Child Care and Development Centers, Inc.

The toughest part was that health department people and the

licensing people came by and said that the trailer was too close to the road and too close to a little creek. They said that we had to move it. During that time, the White Oak Clinic operated out of a trailer. One morning it burned. Immediately we asked the clinic people to sublease the land to us if they weren't going to use it anymore. They couldn't sublease it, but they suggested we talk with the coal company. We went and leased that place and set our trailer there. The fire marshal and the licensing and health department people came and said they would only approve the trailer for six months. After that we would need to have a building. But we didn't have any money.

In 1974 a reporter came up from Nashville and wrote a little piece in the paper about our work and our struggles. Someone down below Nashville read it and called me and said he'd heard that we needed a building. He told us that he had built this double-wide trailer (the schools were buying a lot of them then for the extra programs they were getting started), and somehow it happened that the people who had ordered it didn't take it. He gave us a deal on it where we didn't have to put any money down. We bought it on a lease-purchase plan, where all the money we paid went to our purchase of the trailer. We got the payment approved as rent through the Tennessee Department of Human Services, so we could put the payment in our budget. For three years we paid on that trailer in that way. It held twenty-five children; the first one was licensed for eleven.

During that year, a person from the Commission on Religion in Appalachia brought a woman visitor from American Baptist Women. After being there part of a day, she asked what our greatest need was. I said, "More space, because there are many more children who need to be here, but we don't have the space." She went back and raised a $12,000 grant through her organization and sent it to us through the CORA office.

At the same time, a friend I'd grown up with moved to Jellico from her little house in White Oak because she wasn't able to take care of it and wanted to sell her four-room block house and acre of land. In May 1979, we bought that little house and the one acre for $7,500 and renovated it with the remaining funds from the grant. In July 1979, the building was licensed under the name "Little House Freedom Center" for twenty-six children. We had been limited by space before, and now we would be freed to serve children the way we wanted and needed to.

We operated both centers until November 27, 1979, when our double-wide trailer burned, about four o'clock in the morning. The fire destroyed the trailer and all the records, furnishings, and equipment. Congressman John Duncan organized a meeting with head persons of government agencies to see what each could do to help out. The Appalachian Regional Commission approved an emergency grant to purchase equipment and fencing for a new playground.

We had to immediately find space for the twenty-five children who were being served in the trailer when it burned. We didn't have space in our new little building. The White Oak Clinic group came to our rescue once again. They let us use the clinic building for a child care center. And once again, licensing standards only allowed us to stay there for six months with our twenty-five children.

We paid off the trailer, and with the insurance money we got, about $4,000, we started building on to the little house we had bought so we would have space for the children who were being cared for at the clinic building. We were soon running out of money. We thought that we could finish renovating our building if we had $7,000 more. We went to the bank and talked with the bank president about a loan. He told us that we could get one and that he would send somebody up to look at the building.

Meanwhile, the unseen hand was busy, and the Great Spirit was paving another way for us. About a year before, we had applied to the Presbyterian Women's Giving Fund for a $10,000 grant. The same day we spoke to the banker about a loan, one of the staff, Shirley Cox, got the mail. I was running around trying to get some things done when she said, "By the way, you got a letter here from the Presbyterian Women." I looked, and there was the $10,000 check. It came just at the time we needed it most.

With that money, we finished the building. I designed it, with help from the East Tennessee Design Center. A women's construction crew, sponsored by Mountain Women's Exchange (based in Jellico), helped with the building. Children helped clean and paint. We worked all winter to add on to our building so we could have all the children under one roof. We built a lunchroom (of course, the lunchroom was used as a classroom, too) and a kitchen, and we added some bathrooms. There was enough space in the total building for sixty-two children. All the children were there as of about May 1, 1980.

In 1988, with help from the Save the Children Federation and several churches, MCCCDC acquired eighteen acres of land, half flat bottom land, the other half hill land. Plans are being developed to build a new child care facility and playground on part of the flat land. The new child care center will accommodate sixty-two children, like our previous building, and will be built to all state and federal specifications, so it will be easier to license and keep up. We'll then be able to use the older buildings for the other programs we operate.

I'll try to describe a day at the child care center. Around six o'clock in the morning, the bus driver, with his aide, goes on the bus and starts the long journey down the winding mountain roads to Jellico, to Newcomb, and places about twenty miles away to pick up children. This is not an ordinary school pickup. It's for children from babies three months old, sometimes younger, up to six years old. They pick these children up all along the way, and they buckle them in their little seatbelts and in their infant chairs. The young woman who is the bus aide takes such good care of the children on the bus. It's a big responsibility. By the time they get all the children gathered up, the bus is really loaded, and they come back up the

Some of the child-care-center staff: from left, Lora Leach, June Pyle, Betty Kemplen, Ann King, Tilda Kemplen (with one of the charges), Barbara Jane York, Georgia Morris, Patricia Bolton (Warren Brunner)

mountain and get to the day care center about fifteen minutes of eight, or sometimes eight o'clock, according to how things are on the road.

When the bus backs into the yard, the teachers are already there. They go out, and it takes them about ten or fifteen minutes to carry in all the babies and toddlers. At times we've had up to twenty babies in diapers and just barely big enough to walk and talk, and some are even smaller, so it takes a while. After the children are in the child care center, the teachers take them to their rooms. Sometimes teachers with the older children will have eight or more children, but those with the younger ones have five or six in their rooms. The teachers take off the children's coats and put away their things, then take them and wash them up in the bathroom. If they need diaper changes or anything, they get that.

The cook has been there since 6:30 a.m. getting breakfast ready and getting things ready for the day, and the children are served breakfast. Sometimes they're given cold cereal, but most of the time on chilly mornings they get oatmeal and raisins or some other hot breakfast. It takes a lot of hands to feed twenty children who are not old enough to feed themselves, so everybody is helping to feed those babies, even the maintenance worker and the bus aide and the cook. It's a really neat thing that's happening there in the morning. The older children are eating by themselves, of course, with teachers sitting with them. After they've eaten, the teachers take the older children to brush their teeth.

The teachers have a curriculum they go by. They're doing certain things at certain times. The children learn early in life that they have a routine, which is good for them. The teachers have prepared storybooks, puzzles, blocks, all kinds of things they systematically work with. During the morning, all the children have free play, a time when they're able to go where they want in their space and do what they want to with things set up for them to do. Free expression and play is really important for them. The teachers watch, encourage, and guide, but the children are free.

After that, if the weather permits, they have time on the playground for partially organized and partially free play. They have swings and slides and climbing things to help develop the large muscle skills. The sandbox is a great place to play. The children have lots of pretty things to play with, like their sand buckets. We have red, blue, yellow blocks, all the colors that they need to learn. It's a stimulating situation they're in.

After their outside play, they come back in and get washed up. It's getting along toward lunchtime. The babies are fed about eleven o'clock, and the older children are fed lunch at 11:30. While some of the teachers are getting the babies fed, the other teachers sing or have some other kind of get-together with the older children. The teachers and the children are singing and playing and having a good time. The children experience many things in that one morning.

After lunch they brush their teeth and get ready for bed. It's hard to believe that forty children will sleep at the same time. When the children first come to the center, they don't want to sleep, because they're not used to taking naps in a routine manner, but after about three or four days, they begin to take naps. They'll usually want to take their naps. If they don't, we try to get them to. They sleep for a while, and if any of them get up during the time when the other children are asleep, the teachers have something for those children to do so they're not just milling around. I go through sometimes and get them all up and have them doing things while the others are sleeping. I'll take them off and do things with them, because I enjoy it. Sometimes I take my tape recorder in and play some music. I have a good time with the toddlers.

During nap time, the cook prepares a snack for them (fruit, vegetables, cookies, peanut butter) so they can have it when they get up. The children expect it; it's something they need. We have a good nutrition program. While I'm sure they do get other food, if children who come to our center didn't get any other food during the day than what they get here, they could survive, and they would be well-fed. They get breakfast, lunch, and a snack, and the babies have milk and juice any time they need it. Our food money comes from the U.S. Department of Agriculture, and we've been receiving it since the very beginning. One of the first things we did was to go after funding for food for the children, because good nutrition is so important.

After the children have had their snack, the teachers do things with them that they enjoy, like dancing, singing, exercising, art activities, or whatever else is on the schedule. Then, at 3:30 p.m., the bus comes again, and it takes about ten to fifteen minutes to get them all buckled in their seats. After the bus rolls away, it takes about another hour and a half to get all the children home on that long bus run.

There's no other program anywhere in the area, not even in Jellico, that serves the children in full-day child care, so we bring them out of those areas where there are no services. We would like to see a program like ours in every community so we wouldn't have to carry children so far on the bus, but we've not been able to do that. Getting another building, getting funding for another program is almost impossible now with all the budget cuts and all the things that have happened to day care centers.

When children come into our day care, a lot of times they're not very happy or well-adjusted, and they seem kind of sick or not exactly well. I've referred to them as small rosebuds when they come into the program. After just a little while—for some a few days, for others a month or so—the rosebuds blossom into beautiful roses. We see them happy and healthy, well-fed, well-loved, and well cared for. When I see one child happy, I blossom into a rose, too. I feel that it's worth every bit of effort that's been put forth and all the money that the government and everyone else could put in.

It's so apparent to us that the child care program is good for the children. It's been proven that they are much, much better off than children who are not able to have that kind of care in the early years. As I've said about myself, the very early years are the ones that set the patterns for life, and you never grow out of those patterns.

When the parents see how well-behaved the children are, some say: "They're not that good at home. They're mean at home."

I joke back to them: "We don't have any mean children. We have mean parents."

Some public school teachers have said that the children are troublemakers when they come to school. We've taught them not to sit still but to do things, to have self-expression and be free. Some teachers expect children to sit down, and if they sit down and are really quiet, they're good children, good students. We feel that children have to be active, and they have to be motivated. They need to be able to express themselves as children and to be appreciated for all the little things they do. Even if someone wants to call it being mean, we just feel that they're well, happy, and active, and we like that. We have had some teachers say that the day care children are so different and so far advanced when they come into the classroom that they help the teachers get the other children adjusted to being at school. They motivate them to quit crying and get them pacified.

It seems that most of the children who have gone to our programs and stayed over a period of time do really well in school. They're proud of themselves, and they feel good about themselves. The teachers are not going to put them down. If the teachers would just listen to those children and not want them to sit down and be quiet, they might learn something. If we can listen, and if we can let them have a say in their education, the children will be good teachers.

After they start school, a lot of our children come to visit us and say, "I'm on the honor roll"; that's exciting. We've seen children, my granddaughter being one, who have gone on to graduate from high school; my granddaughter was one of our first day care children. One girl who attended our child care center has finished high school and is now working at the child care center. Many others who attended have done very well in school and have worked in our organization from time to time.

We have continued our summer program, because that was our beginning, our roots, and over the years we've continued to serve the children from the time school is out until it starts again. For the ones who want to come to the center, we try to have volunteers and a ~urriculum; we also have food, recreation, and socialization programs. I'm really proud that we can continue so that the older, school-age children have somewhere to be, too. There isn't much for children in the way of recreation here. We're very limited most of the time by not having enough staff to take care of the children and actually do a good job with them. Sometimes we have as many as thirty or forty around in the summer besides our day care children.

We've also had a summer program for youth, at one time funded by the Comprehensive Employment and Training Act (CETA) and now funded by Job Training Partnership Act (JTPA). The JTPA pays young people fourteen to twenty-one years old to work in a training situation. We train those young people by placing them in our center to help with the child care and greenhouse and gardening work. They work with the school-age children, helping them with educational, recreational, and social activities. They feel important when they're helping other children. It's been a great way for everybody to get involved—children helping children, youth learning to cope with little children. The youth, after all, will soon be young parents.

Funding for the child care center and related activities has been an ongoing struggle. In the early years of MCCCDC getting organized, the Appalachian Student Health Coalition provided us with funds, as well as with students during the summers to help us with the children's programs. The staff of the East Tennessee Research Corporation (ETRC), many of them veterans of ASHC, provided support to our organization by helping us cut through the red tape to get licensed and incorporated in the state and to receive tax-exempt status.

The Campbell County government received federal revenue-sharing funds to help with service programs. Each year we would write a proposal asking for a portion of the funds to operate our child care center. The proposal had to go to the county judge, then to the Campbell County Board of Commissioners. We then had to represent our proposal at a county court meeting. Very little money did we ever get from this source. The judge and all the commissioners were men, and they really resented women who could write a proposal and would come to a meeting and fight for the rights of children or anyone else.

One way we handled the political situation was to get contacts with state and federal agencies and go straight to them with requests for funding. This was easier. We applied to the Tennessee Department of Public Welfare, which had Title IVa funds to support child care programs. We wrote proposals that weren't very professionally done but that got results. The biggest problem we faced with getting state funds was the need for a 25 percent local match. For this we had to call on churches outside the area. Raising money in the local communities was near to impossible because of the economic conditions.

In the early years of organizing MCCCDC, the Appalachian Regional Commission had some funds for child care. We developed a proposal asking them to support the matching portion so we could get the funds from the Department of Public Welfare. They approved a $13,000 grant for the first year of a five-year grant, with a 20 percent reduction each year until the end of five years. At the end of the funding period of five years, an evaluation of the child care program was conducted. The representative who did the evaluation of our center said that all the other centers funded by ARC were no longer in operation. He was pleased to see a program not only operating but growing.

Since that time, assistance to continue and expand has come from a number of sources. Federal sources include Title XX Social Services Block Grant funding from the Department of Health and Human Services and allocated to the state for distribution; the Aid to Families with Dependent Children (AFDC) working mothers program; the CETA program, now replaced by JTPA; Volunteers in Service to America (VISTA), administered by ACTION; and the Child Care Food Program of the Department of Agriculture's Food and Nutrition Service. Private sources include the Save the Children Federation, which provides Title XX matching funds; the Tennessee Federation of Women's Clubs; foundations, including the Ms. Foundation for Women; the Commission on Religion in Appalachia; and individual churches. Those that have provided a continuing support system include Title XX, CORA, Save the Children, the First United Methodist Church of Oak Ridge, Tennessee, the Christ Church of Charlotte, North Carolina, the Church of the Good Shepherd of Lookout Mountain, Tennessee, and the Tennessee Federation of Women's Clubs.

Churches have been very important in supporting the work of Mountain Communities Child Care and Development Centers. In the early years of our work, we got involved with the Commission on Religion in Appalachia. CORA has ministered to Appalachian communities since the mid-1960s. It's a combination of close to twenty denominations working together to make Appalachia a better place for people to live by supporting projects that are trying to help people help themselves in housing, child care, education, jobs, or whatever people need to help them take control of their own lives. As a regional organization, CORA serves as a vehicle to bring churches and community groups into partnership with each other.

CORA raises money from all the different denominations that make up their great network and disburses that money directly to community groups. They have supported our efforts with funds and technical assistance since 1972. CORA provides some of the freest money our organization has ever had. We've been able to do what needed to be done without too many guidelines. You've got to meet criteria to get their money, but you don't feel bound by a set of rules and regulations. You have to do some reporting, but you don't have to tell them everything you're going to do with the money. They expect that you'll do only what you need to do with it.

The CORA process of church working with communities is so different from any other church work that I had seen come into our communities. CORA appreciates the economic and community development that groups are involved in, because they place emphasis on how economic change comes through partnership in ministry. Rather than doing things for people, CORA works as a partner with and advocate for community organizations, supporting their ideas and efforts. It's a lot different from what we think of as church; we know that's what church should be doing. With CORA we know that what we have to say is just as important as what the ministers or the administrators of the national boards of churches say. We can talk about any issue at the meetings, and we're heard. It's a place where we come to share everything.

The other great thing about CORA is the positive attitude of the people involved with the organization. A person from each project is invited to be on one of the committees so that we can come together and share our experiences and our views. We share our stories, ideas, needs, successes, failures, and glories. Everybody tries to help make a success out of unsuccessful efforts. All of us throughout Appalachia have become very good friends, each one knowing and reading about everybody else, and if one has a real success, everyone is happy. When I was asked to go up to New York to give Dolly Parton her *Ms.* Woman of the Year award for her outstanding public service to the local communities in East Tennessee, the whole CORA group was anxiously waiting for me to share that experience when I got to the meeting, because my glory was their glory. It is really great how we have learned to share and love each other and appreciate one another's efforts.

Sometimes everybody begins to work on some of the same things, even though we're many miles apart, separated by creeks, ridges, mountains, counties, and states. One year we realized that every project was working on adult education all over Appalachia. At one of the CORA meetings, our organization learned about Heifer Project International from someone who operates an animal project in Kentucky, and we got funding from that same organization to begin a project in our rural communities. After we got funded, several other projects began to spring up in other parts of Tennessee. It's that chain reaction that has happened, people helping people. The goal is to help people who feel helpless and hopeless gain power over and control of their own lives.

Our organization has been able to work with many, many churches all over the United States, mainly around the region, in Knoxville, Oak Ridge, Chattanooga, Nashville, and North Carolina. We work with all denominations and have both moral and financial support from these churches. It's meant a great deal not to be bound by any church's rules and regulations. When we get support from church organizations, we don't have to go strictly by their standard of what they might see as economic development or education. We do whatever the people need. We've been able to work very effectively with churches, even church organizations in New York City: United Methodist, Presbyterian, Episcopal, United Church of Christ. We've gotten grants from several of the major church groups.

It makes me really happy to be able to be responsive to all church or government agencies, county agencies, all kinds of people who offer something that we can work with, like jobs for people through training or work experience, or a church sponsorship or scholarship. We've always worked with people however they could work with us. We've appreciated whatever they have done or given, if it was a dime or a dollar or many thousands of dollars.

Through word of mouth, our ministry has grown from the early years when it was hard to get anybody to listen to the idea and concept of early childhood education. When we first began, we didn't have any resources except our people resources, and we had to look to agencies for help to get started. John Davis, who was then the director of the Anderson County day care programs, told us a lot of the things that we had to do to legally operate a child care center. He helped us find out who the licensing person was and all the people we had to work with in Knoxville, Oak Ridge, and other places to get through the red tape and be able to operate a child care center.

As we began to talk with people, and individuals heard about our work, they would call to ask if they could visit us to see what we were trying to do. They also wanted to know if they could bring us something when they came. When we got in contact with one person, that person would seem to know some other people who would be interested. Even though we didn't have a facility that could be licensed or anything, they would ask us things like, "Did you know that this church group in Oak Ridge might be of help?"

Our story began to be told. As the local newspapers found out that something was going on, they wanted to come out and do stories. Even some national papers came. I don't know how it all happened, but it did. It's grown to become a great network of people in many different agencies and churches, different women's and men's groups, all over East Tennessee and all over the country who appreciate what we're doing and support it.

Many of the churches we work with have brought their youth groups and adult groups to help us with some of the work that we don't have skilled people, time, or money to do. For several years starting in the mid-1980s, people from the Bethel Presbyterian Church in Kingston, Tennessee, had been coming up periodically to visit the center. One time a group from this church came up on a Saturday morning and brought three vans, one full of clothes, two full of people willing to work. They worked a whole day with me to help us do whatever was needed. They painted, built shelves, put up a television antenna, and helped with the plumbing. We all enjoyed and appreciated our time together.

Sometimes we visited and shared in their church services. After one service, a lady came up and asked if we had a television. I told her that was one thing we didn't have to have, so we'd never put our money into one. Before the Kingston church group came up that Saturday, Dick Hettrick, the pastor, called me to say that they were coming. He said that the lady who had asked about the television had asked her husband to buy one and some other equipment for her birthday. She wanted to give it to the children as a gift for their center so they could enjoy the children's movies and the educational programs on television.

She'd had surgery and couldn't come along, but the group came and brought the gifts. Along with some tapes for children, she sent along a television, a small video camera, and a VCR so that we can make tapes of things the children do and show the tapes back to them; that can be a good learning experience. We appreciated her so much for giving her birthday gift to our children. This surely is Christian love.

This is typical of all the church groups. They like to put not only their money into our work, but they like to come and work with us and put themselves into it. I really appreciate that, because I feel that until you put yourself into something, you can't really appreciate or understand it. When people bring themselves together and share together, they learn to appreciate one another for what each one can contribute. Then they really have a relationship and a network that is good for everyone involved. It keeps good relationships with the churches.

When churches get involved with our organization and when people come to see what's going on and what the needs are, they don't have any problem trying to find a way to help us when they see us working with very limited resources, making the best use of our space and whatever we have. They're anxious to help. The First United Methodist Church in Oak Ridge is one of our greatest sources of church support. Pauline Miller, a member of that church, has been a great inspiration and has helped us with contacts, money, and whatever else she could do for the past fifteen years. Pauline taught children in these mountains in the 1930s during the Great Depression. She taught at Clairfield Elementary School. When she was eighty-six years old, she was given a $50 check by her women's circle to recognize her for her fifty years of service to the Methodist Church and to local communities.

She said she immediately thought, "I know what I'm going to do with this," and she waved the check around, saying to the women, "Guess where this will go?"

They said, "We know—to Mountain Communities Child Care."

Pauline said, "This is going to pay on a new washing machine, because theirs doesn't work, and they have to wash for the children."

Starting with her $50, she didn't have any problem raising $400 to pay for a washer. She's elderly, and her eyes are failing. She couldn't even drive in the mountains. She drove as far as LaFollette, and I went down to help her pay for the washing machine and do the business part of it. We had dinner together and had a good time. The washing machine was delivered a few days later. Pauline has been one of our greatest supporters. Because of her and the others who support us, we know our ministry will never die.

For many years we have worked with Save the Children's Appalachian program, based in Berea, Kentucky, on sponsoring children. While we do most of the sponsorships through Save the Children, several years ago we decided that we might start our own little sponsorship program through our child care center's contacts with churches, groups, and individuals. Our Sponsor a Child project has become a really good way to match families with people who need somebody to be responsible to and for. It's a way for people to identify with particular children or families and become friends with them and write to them, visit with them, and buy them gifts at Christmastime.

A lot of church groups, Sunday school classes, women's groups, and individuals sponsor a particular child. Many members of the Tennessee Federation of Women's Clubs sponsor children through our program. We set sponsorship money at $240 a year, which wouldn't even take care of a child for a month, but with several people sponsoring children, it makes up a good bit of our budget. Sponsors receive a photograph and biography of the child as well as information about the family. They are encouraged to correspond with and get to know the child personally.

I feel strongly that with the budget cuts in children's programs, we would never have been able to survive had we not gotten support from a lot of churches and organizations and a lot of individuals. If we'd had to depend totally on federal government funding or state funding, our programs would have been gone long ago. One of the hardest things for me was to see what happened to people because of the budget cuts, which have done such an injustice to poor people, the elderly, and children. At one time, we had lots of staff members on CETA programs. We didn't have another way to pay them. We had twelve CETA workers who were caring for the children, working with the greenhouse and gardening, and helping with maintenance and with the bus driving. They were getting good training and were really happy. They were able to survive and keep their families together. One day we got a letter saying that all the CETA programs had been cut off the day before. With one whack of the budget ax, there were twelve people suddenly without jobs.

We even have to find 25 percent to match the 75 percent that Title XX provides. Without other funding, we can't get government funding; we've got to have that matching funding. That's been a hard thing. Save the Children pays our matching money to the Tennessee Department of Human Services, which administers the federal Title XX money. Save the Children can't give us the matching money directly; the state sends it back to us in reimbursement. For any program we get funded, we have to pay the money up front and get repaid on a reimbursement rate. When a small group like ours doesn't have a bunch of money around and doesn't have a big, big program funded, there isn't any up-front money.

So it's been really hard to do a lot of the things we've done. I don't even know if I could explain how we have survived, except that every time it looks as if we're going to have to close our doors or cut off staff, we don't panic. We just hold out and do the best we can, keeping faith that somehow we're going to be able to keep our doors open. We have been able to develop a lot of programs and add services, because we believed that somebody would help us, and someone always has. Down through the years, if there's a time when there's no money and somebody has to be cut off, I take no salary until we can handle the situation better. Sometimes we have to cut off staff and put them on unemployment because we can't handle it when we no longer have money to pay them. It's not the way we like to do things, but we can't help it. But we've never had to let our programs down. We've never had to cut off a service, and we hope we never do.

This is a speech I wrote concerning the budget cuts and how they would affect the programs I was working with. I sent it to members of Congress and the Appalachian Regional Commission in 1980, when the administration started with its proposed budget cuts.

We live and work in the rural, mountainous area of Campbell County in East Tennessee, one of the most beautiful places in the world. It has been and still is rich in natural resources that have helped support the nation and the world with energy. When the unemployment rate is high in Campbell County, it is even higher in the mountains, touching 50 to 75 percent.

Our community-based, nonprofit organization has developed community services and job opportunities for low-income people. Mountain Communities Child Care has worked with churches, foundations, and county, state, and federal agencies developing relationships to bring in services and jobs through VISTA, CETA, Title XX, ARC, USDA, human resources agencies, and any other agencies with opportunities for training and employment for community folks.

Over a period of twelve years we have served approximately five thousand school children in recreation, nutrition, and educational services. We have served approximately two thousand preschool children and offered employment to at least one thousand parents and disadvantaged youth.

The proposed budget cuts of the administration would force us all to see these sources become nonexistent, once again taking away the ray of hope and the self-confidence and pride that people have gained in being able to earn a decent living and contribute to society in their own communities.

I would like to address the conditions that the proposed budget cuts upon service programs would create:

Thousands of parents without jobs standing in welfare and food stamp lines, trying to get help—with no help available. Millions of school-age children eating a cold sandwich if their parents can afford it, many not attending school, because they have nothing for lunch or breakfast— other millions of preschool children being denied the opportunity to have services prior to school age, which denies them the right to good nutrition, health care, love, and attention that is their God-given right. If our national leaders permit all the things to happen that are being proposed by the administration, in a very few years we will have the sickest, most underdeveloped nation in the world while leaders are trying to find a solution.

This is the picture created by all the cutbacks in the budget, most of them aimed at the children, the disabled, the handicapped, and the elderly:

Let us visualize a great pasture all parched and burned by the glare reflected by the budget ax, swung by the strong, young, wealthy, and well-taken-care-of. This pasture is filled to capacity by starving children—starving not only for food, but love, attention, health care, and education, which are the rights to which every child is entitled. It is filled with elderly men and women who have been the salt of the earth, helping to bring this great nation forward, suffering and dying from diseases caused by bad working conditions, created by factors beyond their control, still trying to help others less fortunate than themselves who have been blind, deaf, or handicapped from birth.

Also in this great picture we see a few who have learned they are important, and what they say and do is as important as what the great leaders say and do. These people stand up for what they believe in. They try to be heard by people who have the power to make decisions and hope they will respond to these needs before it is too late.

We hope that everyone reading this, especially people who have the power in their hands to do something about the situation, will look closely at what we have said. When you think of the dollar being spent on rural Appalachian services, try to look beyond the dollar bill, and instead of seeing the face of one of the presidents, try to see a child who, without the support of these programs, would never have the opportunity to grow up in an environment where the necessities of life—health care, nutrition, education, and job opportunities—are present.

OTHER COMMUNITY SERVICE PROGRAMS

Over the years, Mountain Communities Child Care and Development Centers, Inc., has developed a number of community service programs in addition to the child care center. We operate many of these projects out of the old Eagan Elementary School. We call it our "creative learning center." We leased this abandoned four-room brick school building from the owner, the J. M. Huber Corporation, the large landowner in the area that bought out much of the American Association land. The Huber Corporation, which has been generous to nonprofit organizations in the area, donated $12,000 for renovations.

A variety of other organizations have helped provide space for our community service programs. Save the Children provided the plans and funds for putting in a fence, furnace, bathrooms, new ceilings and floor tiles, kitchen lights and equipment, tables, and chairs at our Eagan center. Ball Camp Baptist Church in Knoxville also helped out. Early on, the Tennessee Valley Authority donated a trailer, which serves as a community library, adult education classroom, and emergency food pantry. The trailer sits by the child care center in White Oak. The Tennessee Federation of Women's Clubs gave financial support to fix up the trailer and supports our work by collecting food, clothing, seeds, and school supplies.

One of our key community service programs is the prenatal program I had always wanted to develop to help mothers bring forth healthy children by having good nutrition, good prenatal care, and good education about self-care. It took a long time for it to happen. About twelve years after our efforts started, the Center for

Health Services at Vanderbilt University got in touch with the Ford Foundation and found out that it was funding a program for prenatal care in rural areas, especially in places that didn't have clinics. The clinics in our area had closed down because of problems with funding or management.

They asked us if we wanted to write a proposal for a prenatal care project. They said: "You've got to gather a lot of facts and figures about your area. Can you do that?" We gathered all the required information, including the number of doctors in the area, how many people got prenatal care, how many babies were born alive, and birth weights. After we got our material together, we submitted our proposal to the Center for Health Services so that it could integrate it with proposals from other communities. With Ford Foundation funding, the Maternal and Infant Health Outreach Worker Project (MIHOW) came into being. It gave us the opportunity to do the things that we had always wanted to do to help mothers bring forth healthy children who would not be undernourished or retarded or suffer from any of the other things that can happen when mothers don't have proper care and nutrition.

We have worked with this project since December 1982. We started out to recruit ten high-risk expectant mothers the first year. In the first six months of our work, we had twenty-six mothers who were expecting babies. Expectant mothers are the most beautiful of women. Some of them had never been to the doctor and might be four or five months pregnant. We helped them get appointments with doctors and helped them get benefits from Women, Infants, and Children (WIC), the federal supplemental nutrition program. We talked about self-care and the importance of eating the right kind of food. If expectant mothers smoked or drank, we encouraged them to cut down. It was a long, hard struggle, but we showed them the facts and figures of what smoking or drinking can do to unborn children. The mothers, especially the young ones, were willing to try to cut back. Many of them would quit doing things they thought would harm their babies, and they ate things they didn't even like to try to help bring better health to their children.

Sometimes young parents in our area get married, and sometimes they don't. The systems have been geared against family life instead of helping families stay together by creating jobs for people so they can work and be proud of what they do. There's a real incentive for young people not to get married when they can't get jobs and can't support the baby, including paying the expensive hospital and doctor bills. If they can't support the family, sometimes they decide to not get married so the young woman can get a medical card. A lot of times parents have had to separate, and sometimes they've gotten divorced so that the woman could get welfare or a medical card. There's now been a law passed that if a young man doesn't have a job and there's no money coming into that home at all, the mother and the children can get a medical card even if the couple is married— at last, an effort to keep the family together.

We've worked really hard to try to help families hold together and not have to separate. Sometimes people don't know that there are services available to them, like medical cards and other things they have rights to. The MIHOW workers have been very instrumental in helping families find out what resources are available to them and helping them get appointments to apply for these resources: maybe from WIC, maybe through a Medicaid card or from a health department program they need to know about. Sometimes we go with people to help them apply for what is rightfully theirs in the way of services and resources. We've even helped people find ways to get housing in the Housing and Urban Development (HUD) projects in the towns. We didn't like to do that and have them move away from their communities, but sometimes there was nothing else we can do. At least we helped them find a way to get into decent houses with their babies instead of having to live just anywhere.

We didn't have any resistance from the mothers about the project as we went to talk to and work with them, because they felt a need for someone to talk to. A lot of young mothers didn't know who to turn to about their situations. They were glad to have somebody come and act as a friend and neighbor to them and be concerned about them.

As we went into the homes, some of the young fathers didn't understand why everything wasn't all right just as it was and why we were coming to talk to their wives. The wives would tell us that their husbands would rather we wouldn't come. One of the things we tried to do was to get the fathers' approval by asking them to be there. We included them by getting some portable video monitors and showing tapes on many things that both the mothers and fathers wanted and needed to know, including birth control, birthing of the child, and breast feeding. The fathers became more interested when they could see that we weren't doing anything to put them down or cause them to feel that somebody thought they weren't doing their part by their wives.

The fathers have become more involved in the pregnancy and the birthing process. Both parents attend childbirth classes, and the fathers go to the hospital for the birth. A long time ago, when I was having my children, most fathers didn't seem to understand that their role was to support the wife. In earlier years, the men had to work out in the coal mines and other places. They were gone most of the time. I guess they were as supportive as they could be. My husband did go to the hospital with me.

Children don't come into this world able to take care of themselves, so the parents are there to guide their lives and to nourish them, to teach them from the very beginning. Even before children are born, you're taking care of them through the way you think and act. They need to feel safe and secure and feel the love and care you have for them so they come into this world wrapped in a blanket of love. I know it's a shock when they leave the mother's body and come into the world. You've got to help them through that shock. I feel that the family has to be really loving and caring. The love that the mother and father and siblings provide is what shapes a child's life. We all do things without thinking, especially children. They don't know they shouldn't do something until after they've done it. If you discipline children with love instead of disciplining with bad criticism, you don't make them feel that they've done something really bad.

After babies are born, the MIHOW worker takes a well-planned curriculum into the home to help the mothers learn how to do child development activities with the children according to the age of each child. The children are tested every six months to see if they're coming up to where they should be on their developmental skills. There's a curriculum that goes along with the tests. The MIHOW worker takes things into the home to help the mother bring the child along, including colorful story and picture books, educational games and toys, and things for the mothers to make with the children. She also helps the mothers to get the children's well-baby visits and immunizations started. She works with the mothers until their children are two years old.

Our Maternal and Infant Health Outreach Worker Project started with one worker for each project area. I was that worker for our area. I immediately found another worker to help me when our job of recruiting and working with ten people the first year turned into working with twenty-six people. It was much more than one person could do to travel over the rough terrain to visit all those people and try to do all the things we needed to do with them. I was the first one of the five MIHOW workers in the region who found a "natural helper," somebody who could be trained along with me so that she could take over some of the MIHOW work. We could then cover all the areas we needed to. The Center for Health Services itself then began to talk about a program based on the natural helper concept and encouraged each MIHOW person to recruit and start training people who could do the same things we were doing.

We didn't try to find people who had college degrees or nursing degrees, because that wasn't what they had to have to be able to go and be a neighbor and friend to the mothers. They just had to care. We talk a lot about how a "degree of caring" is worth more than a degree in education or psychology or anything else. We can take and have taken many young mothers, even the clients in the program, and trained them to be the workers to go out and help others. They learn by working alongside the outreach worker. We've found ways to give them small stipends to help them take care of their families. We don't believe anybody should be asked to go out and volunteer when they don't have a way to put food on their table and make ends meet at home. We have gotten stipends from United South and Eastern Tribes, Inc., for people with American Indian heritage for a training period of a thousand hours or six months. We have found many ways to pay them after the training period is over. For example, Save the Children has helped us pay one person for a year.

The staff has become very educated—community educated—by doing things in the communities and by becoming beautiful workers, whom I liken to buds that blossom. The young mothers have also blossomed beautifully. One of the things we do with them is have group sessions where they can all come together. At first they might be timid and feel that they don't have much to say in the group. But by the time we get them doing things together, each one says she felt the same way the others did. They get to be friends and neighbors, and they begin to make things work. We don't have to worry too much about who does refreshments or cleans the room or leads the session; they take it on themselves. They are in control of what they're doing, and they're happy about it.

We're really proud of MIHOW. It's been a great economic element of our communities. At this time, we have about six people paid to work in the MIHOW project serving a really big area of our mountain communities. The statistics coming from research we have done throughout our program have shown a big impact on the health of mothers and their children. Breast feeding has increased,

Some of the staff of the MIHOW Project, the toddler program, and the
Substance Abuse Prevention Program: from left, Melaine King,
Melinda Gulley, Shirley Bragg, Teresa Leach, Katherine Gosnell,
Jami McKillop, and Tilda Kemplen (Warren Brunner)

which means better nutrition for the children. The mothers' health
is better, and birth weights are much higher than they were. We've
seen a real improvement in infant survival. Earlier the infants here
had a much higher mortality rate than the state average; now Campbell County has a lower rate than the state average. The prenatal
care the mothers get is a big factor. We have a research document
with all these facts and figures that is public information.

I can't stress enough the importance of the self-care the women
learn, including good nutrition. You can't go in their homes and take
care of them. If you can help them learn self-care, they take care of
themselves. They've learned that for life. It's not something they're
going to forget if they have another child. Not only that, but they
can transfer all this information to any person they come in contact

with. That's another area where we've seen a big impact: women helping women, saying, "This is what I do," or "This is what I've been told to do."

In the early years we had to find the clients who needed services. Now the clients find us. They have learned that there's something good going on that they need. They call us now; we don't have to call them. The hardest thing has been keeping up with the clients, because of their moving around so much due to the lack of affordable housing. You might have a client in one community this week, and next week they have to move out of that house to another one.

Before we came to the end of our sixth and final year of MIHOW funding, we wrote a proposal to the Tennessee Department of Human Services to try to acquire funding for a child abuse prevention program, which would continue with MIHOW clients. We were fortunate to get this program approved. In our first year of funding, 1988–89, we were very successful in working with young families in a home visiting program, helping mothers learn how to care for themselves before their babies are born and how to care for their children. Teen parents and parents-to-be were shown films on family planning, birthing, breast feeding, and child development. Books, pamphlets, toys, games, teaching supplies, and training were provided to help young people—many of them little more than children themselves—cope with being parents. The program was approved by the Tennessee Department of Human Services for 1989–90, and we hope there will be ongoing funding from the state.

When the children were two years old, we had to exit them from the MIHOW program. When one mother left the program, another expectant mother entered, and we carried her through until the child was two years old. We used to wonder what would happen after that with the mother and the children and the rest of the family. We didn't know what we could do for them.

Then, in 1985, a foundation from over in Holland, the Bernard van Leer Foundation, came to see the people at the Center for Health

Services. This foundation was looking for a way to fund something to help children in the United States. I met with its people and was later told by the Center for Health Services director that if I hadn't been at the meeting that day, she didn't know if we would have gotten the funding, because I sold them on the idea that we needed to serve these children on to an older age. Van Leer met with the other MIHOW groups doing prenatal care and funded each one of our sites for three years, $12,400 per year, to hire one more full-time outreach worker to work with families with children two to three.

We've always been concerned when a child had to leave our programs. We've wondered if there would be any continuation of that learning situation. Now I have an idea that we need to carry our children to school age in an outreach program. I don't know where we're going to find that money, but if everything works like it has down through the years for us, I think that will come. A dream might take years, but it happens.

We have had food and clothing programs since the start of our organization, with help from Save the Children and various churches. These programs developed further as we worked with MIHOW clients. We were going out and talking with mothers about good nutrition. We'd take booklets, pamphlets, and films that told them what was good to eat and what was not good, how much of this to eat and how much of that. They said: "We can't afford anything else. We just have to eat what we have." So we thought that if we were going to tell them to have good nutrition, we had to help them get it. People without jobs can't get everything they need. If they receive food stamps, they only last about three weeks out of four. The final week of the month, people are going to food banks or to food pantries, wherever there is food available, to get some supplementary food.

Campbell County got a grant in the mid-1980s to supply food

pantries and to provide some assistance with electricity, heating, and rent for low-income families. We didn't get to participate in the Campbell County Emergency Food Fund program the first year because we didn't know that we could. Either our people were left out, or they had to go all the way to LaFollette or Jellico, about twenty miles each way and, for some people who live way back in the mountains, a lot farther than that. People who didn't have transportation had to hire somebody to take them to the food pantry. They could have taken that money and bought food with it and been just as well off. So we went down to the county meeting and demanded that we get a portion of the food money so we could supply people with food without them having to go so far. Since 1986, we've been part of the county's emergency food program and have disbursed food pantry supplies to low-income and no-income families when they needed it, on an emergency basis.

By going to SHARE Food Bank in Knoxville, we could get additional food to stock our pantry, but we couldn't always get as much of the staple foods as people needed. So we tried to do a better job of going to different places to get food to stock our food pantry for people who said they needed food or didn't have everything they needed for a good diet. One church in Atlanta gave us money to supply the food pantry so we could help families that needed it the most. Each Monday someone from the Fountain City Presbyterian Church in Knoxville picks up bread, cakes, and other food items donated by a Kroger store in Knoxville. The church people bring us the food, and community people and staff distribute it to families. Sometimes one person will deliver to three or four families.

Each Thanksgiving we have a community dinner for everyone who can come to our center. Children, parents, grandparents, great-grandparents, and other community citizens whom we call "the young at heart" attend the dinner. Our dinner consists of the traditional turkey with all the trimmings. Almost everyone brings a covered dish. The specialty is "old fashioned fodder beans" (dried string beans that are cooked). We also have chicken and dumplings, cornbread, pumpkin pie, and a variety of just plain, good food. Often 150 to two hundred people attend. For those who are not able to come to the center (including senior citizens and the sick), our staff, young people, and others take Thanksgiving baskets to them. We often prepare and deliver a hundred baskets containing enough food for a dinner. Each Christmas we make up fruit baskets for the older citizens and people who are sick. They are distributed by the staff, young people, and some of the older people. The Thanksgiving and Christmas baskets are provided by a lovely family in Knoxville.

From the very beginning, we realized that we needed to help people do a better job of gardening, canning, and preserving food so they could have food for their families. We knew that it was better to help a person with some seeds to plant in the spring than it was to give them a box of food whenever they got in really bad shape. If they raised their potatoes and canned their foods, they could eat whether they had jobs or not.

We learned that as a result of industrialization, out-migration and in-migration, and the frustration of it all, people in our area had lost the art of gardening. They hadn't kept up with the good gardening habits and the canning and preserving skills they used to have. Many of the young people were not able to get those skills, because they lived where they couldn't have a garden. We knew from having grown up gardening that the way to always have food was to raise your own.

With help from the East Tennessee Design Center and several churches, we started out in 1979 with a solar greenhouse attached to our child care building. It was the first solar greenhouse in the whole area. It supplied 60 percent of the heat for our building. We hoped the greenhouse would help people understand that they can conserve energy and grow fresh food rather than depending on energy from TVA and the coal companies, fruit from California, and potatoes from Idaho. People don't realize what they've already got.

Patricia Bolton and Tilda learn about plants in the greenhouse
(Warren Brunner)

We raised plants in the greenhouse for the people in the communities and for other groups who were trying to raise gardens.
We were able to raise better plants than people could go out and
buy, and at a cheaper price. We've provided seeds and plants to as
many as 150 families. If they can't pay for them at all, they get them
anyway. The new freestanding greenhouse was built in 1988 with
financial support from Roane State Community College (in Harri-
man, Tennessee) and technical assistance and financial support from
Save the Children. Its purpose is to raise good quality plants for
family gardens in the communities and for our small farms program.
We have a garden at our child care center to provide better, fresher
food for our children, especially during the summer.

When we started the MIHOW program, some of our first contacts were when a neighbor would call us and say that some expectant mother needed food. When we visited her, sometimes we'd find out that her family had just moved in and needed other things in addition to food to take care of themselves. So we would try to get some food to them, along with whatever else they asked for. Most of the mothers said they didn't have baby clothes or maternity clothes. People have to have a good chunk of money to buy them. So we'd tried to get baby clothes and maternity clothes, especially through church groups that would ask us what we needed. We'd tell them that was one of our biggest needs. A lot of young women's church groups have had baby showers for us and sent us whole boxes full of baby clothes that would last a long time.

We have a little store at the child care center where we have good, used clothing for all ages. We try to hold on to our baby clothes and maternity clothes for the mothers we work with, but we have clothing of all sizes that people can come and buy for five or ten cents or a quarter. Nothing in our store ever costs more than fifty cents, and if people can't buy the things they need, they get them anyway. That's a big help to people, because with the prices you have to pay at the stores, even with a pretty good job you can't afford too many clothes. When people have a lot of children, they can't buy much. Sometimes people also get things at our store to make quilts.

We try to always have some children's clothes around for school-age and preschool children. It's really important to have them for the preschool children, because many of our children might have wet clothes by the time they get to the day care center, or they might get sick and vomit on their clothes. Because we deal with such young children, we just have to have fresh clothing for them. If we didn't have a supply of clothes for those children, we'd be in really bad shape.

Usually our clothing comes from churches or women's groups that are working to try to help in our communities. Most of them come from churches around Knoxville and Oak Ridge, Tennessee.

We share our clothing supply with a lot of other organizations if anybody needs them. If we get two truckloads and somebody needs one of them, we give it to them so they can share the clothes in another community.

As we carried out our work, we realized the need for our involvement with substance abuse prevention. In the past few years, drugs have become a very big problem with the young people in the area because of the economic conditions here, with nothing for the young people to look forward to. From what I hear, even the grade schools have lots of drugs being passed around. In high schools, of course, it's really bad, not only here but everywhere. The only organized activity for older children or young people is school. Just going to school isn't enough for children; they need something to balance that. I think they would be better educated if they had something organized for recreation and for taking on some responsibility for doing things. We try to do that during the summertime, but we can only do it for so many children.

I would like for this community to have something for the kids. The biggest thing they have is basketball over at my daughter's house. In the summertime, there are ten or fifteen in Chris's yard most of the time. Not a lot of people have their yards open for all the kids in the community to come and play basketball, but Chris does, and I always did, because we know there's nothing else for them. We'd rather have them in the yard playing than out on the road somewhere, maybe getting into things that they wouldn't need to be into, like drugs and alcohol. I would like to see young people have such a full life and so much to do that they wouldn't need to be influenced by anything harmful to their bodies or minds.

MCCCDC initiated a program for drug and alcohol abuse prevention called Bright Futures. There are no Alcoholics Anonymous or Al-Anon groups here in the mountains, but we started having some meetings in 1987. At our first meeting, we had thirty-five people come out to talk about alcohol and drugs and substance abuse prevention. Many people talked about themselves and their experiences with husbands, wives, and children. Our organization started these meetings, and we hope that they will be going on from now on, that people will come out and support each other in their efforts to reduce the problems.

In 1988, we developed a proposal and sent it to the Tennessee Department of Mental Health and Retardation; money had been allocated because of the Governor's Task Force on a Drug-free Tennessee. Our proposal was approved for a one-year demonstration project to set up meetings with community people to share ideas and create community awareness of the problems. After the first year of funding for a demonstration program, money was allocated to extend the program for one more year. We would like to see this as an ongoing program.

We developed a Just Say No program with day care children and staff, school-age children, young people, and older people. Our young people put up posters and flyers at public places, including the schools. Our teaching was targeted toward children ages five to seventeen. A number of agencies have been very instrumental in the success of our program. Both Campbell and Claiborne County law enforcement agencies have become very involved with our meetings, along with the Just Say No organization in Knoxville and the Koala Center, the drug and alcohol abuse treatment center of the Methodist Medical Center in Oak Ridge.

The Bright Futures program has sponsored a number of special events. In 1989 we had a Halloween carnival at the old Eagan school. Staff of all our projects worked with the young people of the area to develop many activities, including a spook house, fortune telling, an old country store, and an old-fashioned marriage booth. The focus of the carnival was a red ribbon campaign for a drug-free Tennessee. All four hundred people who came to the carnival had the Bright

Futures program explained to them and were given red ribbons to wear. The next month we held a pizza party at the child care center dining room for youth, parents, and children.

In 1990 a Valentine's party was cosponsored by the staff of the substance abuse prevention and child care programs for all the day care children and their families. On the Saturday night following Valentine's Day, a Valentine's dance was held at the old Eagan school for all children, youth, and their families. A youth band from the community provided the music. Refreshments and door prizes were provided by the Bright Futures staff. All these and other activities are to make people aware of the Bright Futures program and to provide something enjoyable for people in the community to do together.

In all my work, my focus has always been education first. I feel that education is something that not many people will be scared of or think of as something bad. If you're talking about classes where you can teach children, or classes where you can teach people to read and write and help them get their high school diploma, or even college classes, that's something that people like.

Adult education has been a strong theme throughout our ministry. The educational status in the counties we serve is very low. The older the people are, the less education they have. I can understand that because of my not being able to go to high school when I got through elementary school. Most people were just like me. They lived back in the mountains, and they didn't have any way to get out and go to high school. If you got a good eighth-grade education when I was going to school, you were lucky. And now, the principal of Jellico High School has said that for every two children in our area who start first grade, one drops out before the end of high school.

Since the planning stages for developing and operating a child care program, we've sponsored adult classes. When we first began trying to develop a child care center, we were told that we had to have trained staff. I asked the licensing person if there was a way to train my own staff. I was told that I could only do it through some school. So I went to the vocational school in Jacksboro to ask if they had a program in child care. They said they didn't have a teacher. I asked if they would help me set up a child care program with a curriculum and let me teach the workers. They said it sounded good, so we worked together to follow through with this plan.

That was the beginning of our organized adult education. We had those classes before we had a place for them. We did some of them out in the fields and some at people's houses—wherever we could meet. Three hours was the limit for classes each night; they lasted ten weeks. The women got certificates for attendance, which gave them so many hours of child care and child development classes, and that was sufficient to get started. Then we had ongoing, on-the-job training classes. To keep the training going, we also got somebody from Roane State Community College to come to our center to teach some classes in child care.

Through having a child care center and working with children and parents, we realized what the needs were. Even though we set up a child care center for the younger children, parents still had older children who had missed out on preschool education, and somehow these children couldn't cope with school; they were getting further and further behind. Parents who didn't have any education couldn't help their children at home. There were many parents who wanted to study so they could help their children with their school work. Some needed to learn to read and write; others needed to learn the new math.

We began to work on some basic education classes for people who hadn't finished eighth grade. I was teaching then. I worked with the school system to set up classes in our child care center at night. I had lots of people, including parents, sixty-year-old women, and

Tilda teaching an adult education class. The students, seated from left, are Ann King, Lora Leach, and Barbara Jane York (Warren Brunner)

teenagers who were fourteen to sixteen years old. I had a whole trailer full every night that we had class. It was a great beginning of adult education.

As systematically as possible, we've continued to have adult education classes over the years. We've had workshops on the Cherokee language, the arts, and other topics. We've run basic education and General Equivalency Diploma (GED) classes for those who dropped out of high school. Many people have wanted to learn to read and write. Some have wanted to study just to feel good about getting a better education. Their purposes have all been different. Our door has always been open to anybody who needed help with something. They have come to our center and found someone there who could help them with whatever they needed to study.

It used to be that when I got a class going, I had to teach it. Now when I get a class going, I get somebody else to teach it; that's a big step forward. Lots of women have gone through classes we've taught and are now setting up classes for community people. People feel good about neighbor teaching neighbor.

Teaching adults is a little hard, because you're apt to think that adults learn the same way children do. That's wrong thinking. You have to be sure that you always keep yourself tuned in to what they want to learn and the way they want to learn it. Children usually try to learn what you lay out for them or whatever you prepare for them; they'll be interested in what you're interested in. You find that adults have their own interests and agendas and their own views on things. You can't teach them the way you do children. You've got to help them the way they want you to.

I don't believe you can actually "teach" adults. You simply make it possible for them to learn on their own. You have to guide them and let them do the work. You have to work on a low educational level and with high standards for them, because they've learned how to do things. They may not have an education in a formal way, but they have come through many years of life experience. And experience being the best teacher, what they need is to learn the value of what they already know. Their life experiences are worth more than anything they'll ever learn from a book, but sometimes they have to learn out of that book how to pull their life experiences together and put them to work.

Getting an education means you can do things that maybe you wouldn't have been able to do. You can take a job that maybe you wouldn't have been able to get otherwise. It looks good when you apply for a job if you have a piece of paper that says you have earned a degree. What it meant to me to get a college education was that I had credentials that would allow me to do the things I wanted to do. It wasn't that I learned so much in college; I learned some things that helped make my life experience more meaningful. But the purpose of it has been that it allowed me to teach school, to work with children, and to set up programs. Credentials are very important to society and to the systems. I don't think credentials make you a good teacher or a good administrator or anything. They just allow you to do it.

Education is a word that's used quite loosely. My idea of education is that from the time you're born until you die, you're being educated, and the purpose is to learn to do the things that you want to do and see a need for doing. I always want to further my education, but not necessarily by going to a university or research center. I do a lot of research on what's available for people and how they can go about getting what is rightfully theirs in order to meet their needs.

In the early years of our ministry, when people got their GEDs or finished high school, they often didn't have enough self-confidence to try to go to a college campus. We worked with Berea College and Cumberland College to bring college classes to our community. People had a wonderful sense of achievement as they started on their way to a career or a better job. One year there were eight college classes being taught at our child care center. Subjects included English, math, history, health, and child care and development.

At the time I began teaching adult education classes and especially when college classes were taught, the instructors would give assignments to write reports or read certain books. There was not a library anywhere closer than the towns twenty miles away or the colleges, which were several hours' drive away. We established our own library in 1979. We made an appeal to Save the Children for help. They sent out an SOS for books and magazines. The reading materials are still coming.

A few years ago, it didn't cost much to take a college class, but the tuition rose so much that it became really hard for people to pay for their education. People simply couldn't afford to attend classes. With funds coming mostly from the Tennessee Federation of Women's Clubs, we set up a scholarship fund to help pay tuition for those who couldn't pay. Most of the people we work with are low-income enough that they can get federal Pell grants for student financial aid and whatever other grants are out there for low-income people.

Many, many people have gone to college. Helen Osborne, the manager of our Native Herb Products operation, is one of them. Many of the child care center staff have received one to two years of college. One of our teachers, Evelyn King, finished college, as did Shirley Cox, who is no longer with us. Almost all of the staff members have at least one year of college, except the newest people. We've not been teaching college classes for the last few years, because Mountain Women's Exchange has organized a rural education co-operative and contracted with both Roane State Community College and Carson-Newman College (in Jefferson City, Tennessee) to offer extension classes at their center in Jellico. I helped organize Mountain Women's Exchange, and while I'm no longer a board member, I support all their efforts.

In the beginning, mostly women took advantage of adult education. Now there are lots of young men in the classes that Mountain Women's Exchange has organized. The men were just a little slower than the women to move into things. I think men feel that people look down on them if they don't have an education or if they don't have a job. Both of those things together could make a man feel pretty inadequate. If there is no work for him here, and if he doesn't have an education to go away from the area and get a job, he's in a really tough situation. That's why we're struggling so hard to try to bring both education and jobs to the area.

Illiteracy is a big problem in our area as well as many other parts of Appalachia, and it's always been a big problem. We didn't realize how bad it was until we started classes in basic education. I thought everybody could read; I thought everybody my age could anyway. I knew my parents didn't have much of a formal education, but I thought everybody my age went to school; that's not true. When we did a labor survey, we saw that the low educational status of both the young and older people is staggering. It's amazing how many people don't have a high school diploma, and a lot of them have less than an eighth-grade education. Many people can't read well, even though some of them have gone through high school. If you can't read well, it's hard to do anything else.

In 1987 our organization made a proposal to the federal ACTION program for four VISTA workers, all local women, to go out into the communities and recruit students and tutors to help them study. ACTION approved the proposal, and this program linking students with tutors operated for several years. Through this program and our other adult education work, approximately five hundred students have worked to further their education. Twenty-six have acquired GED certificates. Some have entered college, and others hold better jobs. And everyone feels better about themselves.

Nobody can go out and take a job that requires a certain skill if they don't have it. Not many employers have a training program to teach you a skill, and if they do, you have to pay for it. In 1987 MCCCDC sponsored a series of multicrafts training classes. Forty-five men and women were trained in building construction, electrical wiring, plumbing, welding, and concrete and steel work. About half of the students didn't have high school diplomas. Two GED classes were taught at the same time so they could work toward their GEDs. The training program was held at the old Eagan School and was paid for by Walters State Community College (in Morristown, Tennessee) and Roane State Community College. The multicrafts training was done by Daniel Construction Company of Greenville, South Carolina. United South and Eastern Tribes paid each participant a training allowance and paid one person to teach the GED classes. The participants helped build the new greenhouse near the child care center. They also built an office and a workshop at the Eagan school site.

Several of the participants later got their GED certificates. Every one of them was offered a job by the Daniel Construction Company. Most of the jobs were so far away that the participants who had families could not take them. Many did go, but found it impossible to support two homes by keeping up a family here with themselves somewhere else. But with the skills acquired through the training, most of the participants have created their own businesses or found jobs more local to them. Not only were people able to get jobs with this training, but they are now able to do repairs in their homes. When they need electricity or water installed, they don't have to pay somebody to do that, they can do it for themselves.

Throughout all my work with adult education, I've not only tried to teach but to learn from everybody I meet. I feel education takes many paths, and that doesn't mean straight to a college campus. It's from you I learn, and from me you learn. And together we teach.

ECONOMIC DEVELOPMENT PROJECTS

There's a big need for jobs in our area. The unemployment rate in Campbell County usually runs around 13 to 17 percent at the Job Service office, and that's only accounting for the people who go to apply for unemployment insurance. The people who have not had jobs don't have anything to apply for, and they're not counted. I've heard the director of the Campbell County Department of Human Services say that when the unemployment rate is 13 percent down at Job Service, it's 50 to 75 percent up in the area where we live. Around 90 percent of the families in the MCCCDC service area live on incomes below the poverty level. In this area of worked-out coal mines, people have felt that there's nothing they could do about their situations and frustrations.

Up until the last few years, some of the men could either get jobs at the surface mines or were hoping they could. That was their goal, to try to get jobs. Many didn't, but they wanted to, and they kept thinking and searching. They didn't want to do the smaller types of things that looked as if they could have been done by women. Their idea of work was not crafts; it was something bigger. Some men were skilled woodworkers. They could whittle and build things. They did a little bit of whittling for the craft shops, but they didn't really want to be identified with the crafts groups.

Believing we had enough wood in the area to support something bigger in woodworking, the Model Valley Development Council tried to organize a woodworking operation in the early 1970s. I don't know where the idea came from to have a pallet factory to make the wooden pallets used to move and store things. The development council had recruited a Robert F. Kennedy Memorial intern to support the efforts of community people in creating an economic development base. The intern researched possibilities, and this one looked feasible. That was one of the things that brought out some of the men and got them into some of the organizing and the decision-making, because they could see that as a man's job. I was on that board of directors.

Our pallet factory only lasted three years, but instead of thinking that it was a loss, I tend to think it was a gain. We had around fifteen men working, and they learned good skills. They learned to be managers, foremen, and good workers. They learned how to go out and market their pallets. Nobody around here had ever had to go out and really market a product before.

Mountain Communities Child Care and Development Centers hired local people to work on a very small basis in the beginning. Whenever we could get a dollar to pay somebody, we would put it into a local person. When people have something in their lives that is beautiful and that they can be proud of, they begin to take control of their lives and to feel good about themselves. When they can do a good, honest day's work, they can come home and feel good about it. And they've helped somebody along the way, because all our work is service. We have to nail nails and dig ditches sometimes, but it all serves a purpose. Those who participate have something to look forward to each day instead of nothing. If I didn't have something to get up for or go to every morning, I'd have this house cleaned up, and I'd still be going crazy. I wouldn't know what to do with myself if I didn't have anything out there that I was reaching for.

Over the years, I've been working and struggling to help revitalize the communities and to do something about the economic development conditions here. All the projects we've tried to develop throughout the years of serving were also for the purpose of economic development, creating jobs, helping people survive where they are instead of having to leave or having to depend on some other source for their income. We've done a great deal of that through our efforts of developing health clinics, child care, maternal health, and the other community service projects. I know people look at them as service projects, but they have actually been economic development projects, since they offer jobs to people in the delivery of services.

The child care center has been the major employer in the area for many years; that's excluding the towns, where there are factories, stores, and schools. Here in the mountains where there are no factories and there is no other employment except coal mining, which is pretty well gone, we are the biggest employer. We now have about thirty-five people employed in the child care center and the other projects we operate. We've offered employment to over one thousand adults and youth through the various programs we've run during the past twenty years.

Lately I've seen some of the men, even some who worked at the surface mines, taking less "masculine" jobs with the service projects. Because the men were used to working in the coal mines, it took some time for them to get into anything that was not traditional, like mining or woodworking. I think that for a long time men may have thought the work we were doing was women's work, but now we have several men working in our organization. I'm really happy about it, especially with the men taking on responsibilities and helping to make things work. They're working with us just however we need to work and are showing real signs of pride and hope in what they are doing.

I don't think that we need to separate things out and say, "This is women's work, and this is men's work," because any of us can do what we set our minds to, if we're physically able. I'm proud I am a woman. Women have had great callings; there have been a lot of great women who have done a lot of great things. I guess we women have taken on jobs that could have been men's jobs. But it's easier for a woman to do a job that could have been a man's job than it is for a man to think he will do a job that a woman could have done, because down through the years some jobs have been identified with women, like school and church. (I don't mean running churches, but organizing things that happen in churches.)

We've gone through some pretty good years when there was work, but when there's not any, people have to learn how to make their living by their own development. It has been impossible to encourage outside industries to bring factories or any other employment here because of the isolation of the area. The rough, mountainous terrain and poor, steep, and curvy roads make transportation difficult. Instead we are helping people to develop their own jobs and also to grow and preserve their own food supply so that they can survive even without full-time jobs. The way MCCCDC has done this is by working in partnership with Heifer Project International, Save the Children, Keep America Beautiful, various churches, and any other organization that can provide support for local people by providing such things as livestock, plants, seeds, and workshops and other training to help them develop their own small businesses or farms.

It's really important to have economic development going on to help families stay together and to make life easier for each family member. I see that with my own family and with a lot of others. The entire family works together, especially on the livestock project and some of our other projects. It's something that has grown out of our not having jobs here and not having the things we've needed. We work to meet the need folks have to become self-sufficient. We give them a hand, not a handout.

Our first major economic development project started in 1985, when we began to develop the Mountain Communities Livestock Project. We work with Heifer Project International (sponsored mainly by churches), which provides animals to low-income families so they can have meat and milk. They can also raise some animals to sell for other things they need. I found out about the Heifer Project at a CORA meeting in Berea, Kentucky, when some people got to talking about how they wrote a proposal and got it approved by the Heifer Project, which then donated animals. I knew that was something we needed to do.

Jim Worstell, on the staff of Save the Children's Appalachian program, gave us an application that day and some information on how to go about working it up. We got it done and sent it to Heifer Project International. We soon got word that it was approved, because our area is one of the lowest in jobs and economic development. It fit perfectly into what we were already trying to do: help people help themselves and stay in the area, in the beautiful mountains we love so much.

This is one of the better projects we've ever been involved with, because it does put food on the table for people, and it has also given people real hope of being able to do something for themselves. The men especially have come out and made this project work. They see the animal project as being something they want to do. Working with the animals is something they have felt really good about doing, although it was started by a group of women and organized under Mountain Communities Child Care and Development Centers. The men see themselves handling the animals, because women always milked the cows and fed the hogs back in the olden times (I always did, too), but as far as managing lots of animals or taking them off the truck and hauling them and breeding them and all that,

Tilda visiting pigs acquired as part of the Mountain Communities
Livestock Project (Warren Brunner)

the men see that as being their job, and they seem to be very happy
with that.

When the men see the animals coming in, they bring out their
old pickup trucks and distribute the animals to the families. One
time four Brangus cows, weighing about a thousand pounds each,
were brought to the community and placed with families. The men
just went out with their trucks and horse trailers and carried them
wherever they were going. They have helped one another birth animals and build fences, barns, and loading chutes. Most of the people
who deliver the animals to the communities and most of the field
representatives (from Arkansas and Kentucky) are men. The men
here have been encouraged to go out and work with them and show
them around the communities, instead of me or some of the other
women going out and having to show them everything (which we
did in the beginning—I've been all over the mountains with them).

The men sort of take on that job now as part of their voluntary service for having this project in the area.

Some of them have started their own animal projects to develop their own jobs. Many of them started feeder pig businesses that could bring income to the family and be their self-sufficiency, their way of making a living and not having to go somewhere and leave their homes and families. Many people were doing quite well at it. Then the price of hog feed went high, and the price of hogs went low. This forced people to get out of the pig business. Then people started raising cows instead. Some people have only two or three cows. A lot of people have gotten cows so they could have milk.

People can also sell off their calves to get money to pay their taxes or get in their coal for the winter or do other things. For several years now, my cow has brought a calf in April. Each year I make enough money selling the calf to pay the taxes on my land, and that's a big help to me. I guess you could call it a business; to me, it's a little business, with one cow. One family near my house runs a little business selling milk from their Jersey cow to neighbors. We are working very diligently with the animal project people to help others like them set up their own small businesses.

We appreciate the beauty of this project, because when a family receives a cow or sow from Heifer Project International, it gives the first female offspring to another family. As families give the gift of love, they make a chain of giving, a chain of life. It's an act of kindness and love that can grow all over the country. It's been a great thing for us to be able to tell the story of our project to other people. We talk about it everywhere we go because it's so important to us, and then other people want to do the same thing. We were the first project in Tennessee, but there have been many other projects developed around other places in Tennessee that are now getting funding from the Heifer Project.

We have gone from not many people having animals to thirty-seven families with animals. Some families that already had animals have gotten additional ones. The emphasis of Heifer Project International is to get good stock into the area so there are good quality animals for meat or for sale. Since the beginning in 1985, we have received fifteen cows, one bull, fifteen sows, and two boars from Heifer Project International.

The Heifer Project donates the actual animals, not money. We have raised some money from churches to help people get their pastures, barns, feeders, and watering stations in good shape so that they could do a better job taking care of their animals. We're still writing proposals to get additional funding. I'm trying to get out from under the directorship of the project, but I want to keep on being the fund raiser because I like talking about it.

The Mountain Communities Livestock Project has been very successful in getting livestock from Heifer Project International and financial support and technical assistance from churches. With a grant from the Presbyterian Committee on the Self-Development of People, we have set up a revolving loan fund for the participating families to use. They can take out emergency loans to meet needs related to their farms and livestock. The loan repayment includes interest, which goes toward helping support the livestock project.

I've liked the people we've worked with, the people who have worked internationally. It's been a great exchange of ideas and a good experience for all of us. They have compared our area to the Third World countries. In 1982 I visited a Third World country myself when I traveled to India. It was a great experience for me. I appreciated seeing the land and the communities. I saw the contrast of the very rich and the very, very poor.

If I had been younger, I might have thought that it would have been good to give a few years of my life to a village in India, maybe in old Delhi. But I made up my mind that when I got back home I wouldn't need to go anywhere else to see what was going on. If I just went somewhere to stay ten days and didn't have a chance to share with many people, there's no need to do that. It's like people coming here to Appalachia and looking at us and going away with an idea of how badly we need somebody.

I knew that a lot of things needed to be done here, that my place was here. There's enough work for me to do at home with my own people to make a better situation. We do share our knowledge with people from other countries. Some have written to ask for my help in setting up standards for economic development projects like the ones I've been doing here.

As our organization kept finding ways to be of service to the community, I became aware that we could assist American Indians in our area. I've been interested in the Indian people all my life. When I was a child, I wanted to be an Indian really badly. I didn't know if I had any Indian heritage or not. I was very concerned about the things I'd read in history books, about how the native people were treated when the white men came to this country and took over their land. I'd always heard about the removal of the native people, their being driven out. I didn't know much about what had gone on and how severe the treatment was until a few years ago when I was in Cherokee, North Carolina, and bought a book about the Trail of Tears. I read that book a couple of times and learned a lot about what had happened to the Cherokees when they were forced to move from the mountains to Oklahoma.

In the area where we live, very close to North Carolina and to the Great Smoky Mountains, many people are Cherokee Indians or their descendants. My husband was about half Cherokee. In the early 1970s, I started trying to identify and collect information about the people of Indian heritage in our area. When I first asked people if they were part Cherokee, people didn't want to talk about their backgrounds and didn't want to be identified as Indian, even to their own children. But some people did begin talking about their heritage. They'd say: "We've always been told that we were part Indian, but we weren't supposed to talk about it at school. We weren't supposed to be identified as Indians, because our parents were afraid of what might happen."

More and more, people began to share ideas and stories about their grandparents and ancestors who were part or full-blooded Cherokee. We got involved with any groups we could that were working with American Indians or advocating for them. Then people began to realize that it wasn't a bad thing to be an Indian, that it was beautiful. People have become very interested in collecting information about their Cherokee heritage, learning more about their ancestors. We've encouraged people to be proud of who they are and to believe in the native ways. We've tried to do things with Indian crafts and education.

The United States government has put together some programs that give American Indians opportunities to work and to further their education. Mountain Communities Child Care and Development Centers was organized as nonprofit; we could apply for CETA jobs through the state of Tennessee. We got involved with an organization, the Tennessee Indian Council, started by one our friends a few years ago, that could apply for funds from the federal government to offer CETA training and jobs to American Indians. We had many, many people working in our organization on those jobs. A few years later, we lost contact with the Tennessee Indian Council. Another American Indian group, United South and Eastern Tribes, was very helpful and instrumental in our keeping staff through their JTPA training program. We were able to get six-month training grants for as many as twelve people in our various projects.

One day I was driving down the road with Bob Hilton from United South and Eastern Tribes. He was coordinating some job development for the American Indians in our area. He told me about a cottage industry project they had tried to start in another community. He said they were not able to get it going. There was a large concentration of full-blooded Choctaw Indians there. The people who ran all the programs and government agencies in that town weren't interested in any programs for the Choctaws. They said: "They're too lazy to work; they're indifferent. They don't want to do anything, and we don't want to do anything for them." So they turned down a government-funded project that would have trained and employed the Indians. I told him that it sounded awful that people would do that.

I described all the things I was trying to do and wanted to see done. We were already trying to raise herbs and make wreaths and do training. We were looking forward to the time when we would have a cottage industry where people could gather native materials to make craft items at home to sell back to the project. The project would then sell the items to craft shops and to people anywhere and everywhere. He said: "That sounds like what we wanted to do in this other community but wasn't accepted. It wasn't the Indian people who didn't accept it. It was the people who call themselves 'white people.' I'm going to tell my supervisor that you've got a project already laid out and cut out for this off-reservation program that we want to do."

We began to work on it in 1982. He wrote up a proposal to the U.S. Department of Labor and got it funded. On my end, I worked with people in our communities to find the land and get all the work done to grow the herbs and the flowers and to gather all the things that bloomed and grew outside that could be gathered and put into the wreaths. We got the project started really well, because United South and Eastern Tribes would pay the people for training through funds from the Department of Labor, and we could coordinate it in the communities. We've had as many as fifteen people working. The men have grown and gathered the herbs; mostly women have made the products. The manager and craftspeople are no longer paid by Department of Labor money, but by their own sales.

Community people had to be identified as being at least one-sixteenth Indian to work at Native Herbs. We found people by word-of-mouth. We think that's the best way for anything to get advertised. After you talk to one person, they'll talk to ten, and it's not hard to find people. It's the same way with a lot of our other projects. If one person comes and finds that we've got food, they'll tell everybody else, and if there's a job or anything going on, everybody tells everybody. We have become a comprehensive creative community learning center where people come for many things.

Native Herb Products has become a cottage industry. People are now doing their work at home and bringing it into the shop. Some people have sold directly to outside markets on their own, which is good. Right now what they're doing is making the wreaths and other products and bringing them into the central place. The project buys their craft items and sells them through whatever marketing resources we have. The items are marketed mainly through Save the Children's craft shops, and there are some being marketed right from the old Eagan school where the main office and training center are located. Many people from all walks of life visit our centers to see the many projects that have been developed and implemented by local people. Hardly a day passes by that there's not somebody at one of our places. When they come to one place, we try to take them to the other one so they see everything that's going on; we sell some of our items that way. We also have some women's groups in Tennessee that are marketing for us. Some of the churches are doing marketing too. In the fall of 1987 our manager brought her display of goods to an Indian powwow in Nashville, Tennessee, to take orders and show our pride in what we are doing with our talents and resources.

While the American colonists brought many herbs with them, the American Indians cultivated other herbs, both medicinal and fragrant, long before recorded history. It seemed especially appropriate to begin again the use of native herbs with people of Indian descent. We've grown many herbs and flowers, including lavender, strawflowers, baby's breath, cockscomb, globe amaranth, sage, thyme, sweet marjoram, tansy, chives, rosemary, and mint. We've also grown yarrow, an herb which is used for medicinal purposes and whose flowers are beautiful to use in dried flower arrangements. Like our ancestors, we have gathered many of our materials from the wild, including rabbit tobacco, pine cones, acorns, and pampas grass.

We couldn't gather enough wild things, and we couldn't grow enough of the basic material to make the hundreds and thousands of wreaths in demand. So we ended up having to buy a product called German statice, a beautiful flower that you see in a lot of dried flower arrangements. The material we bought was grown in Spain, I think, and it was expensive. We tried to raise it, but it takes two or three years to bloom, and it's really hard to keep it growing; maybe we didn't know how. It was easy to work with, but it was hard to keep it from drying out and shedding.

So we turned part of our efforts toward pine cones, beechnuts, nutshells, cotton burrs, and other things that can make a more sturdy wreath. Now that we're doing more of the cone products, they're selling much better, because they're easier to ship and easier to carry and will last a lot longer. Save the Children paid an experienced trainer to come and train the local people to do this craft with pine cones, nuts, buckeyes, and whatever grows wild that can be gathered. She taught them how to cut the cones into little flowerets and arrange them into beautiful wreaths and other products, such as candle rings, candle spirals, and napkin holders. This is the first time that this trainer offered training to a group of people so they could keep that art and these products going. She said there's no way that even a group like ours could meet the demand. The Native Herbs Products manager trains other community people who want to make the cone items.

When our crafts manager, Helen Osborne, got a job through United South and Eastern Tribes to work at the day care, she had two babies, twin boys, and really needed a job. She was young and didn't know which way to go. We helped her get work through a training program, and she worked six months with the children's program. I was trying to manage the crafts project along with a dozen other things, and I couldn't handle it all. So Helen began to work with me and go places with me and see what was going on with the crafts operation. She became very interested in doing it and has been very instrumental in making it grow and become a successful business.

When she started, she said she didn't think she ever could handle it. She didn't feel that her education was adequate for her to take on any kind of management job. I guess she thought that you had to do a lot of book work and paperwork, which you do. She has learned by doing it. Sometimes she has to ask for help on some things, but we all do. The beauty of our ministry is how we help one another to grow in love, wisdom, and faith, each one becoming a support for the others. Helen is very proud of herself for the simple fact that she didn't believe that she could do it, and she has now become a very efficient manager. She is able and willing to go out and work and train others to do the same thing she's done, to help them get to where they believe in themselves and have the energies to put into making their talents work.

When Helen went to the powwow in Nashville, she was happy that she had one of the young ladies who produce the wreaths go along with her, one who has also come a long way with her work, a step at a time. Helen has brought a lot of these young girls along to different occasions and has taken them with her to places they never would have gone outside the area had they not gotten involved with working with Helen. We're really proud of her. When we saw her struggling to make a living, we wanted her to become involved in our work. We knew that she would make a real contribution in our ministry. Helen has a husband; they're both young, and he didn't have a job until recently. Now that he has a coal mining job and she works, they're doing quite well. Their twin boys, who attended our child care center from birth until they were five years old, are very intelligent and are doing well in school.

One time we had to go to Nashville to a United South and Eastern

Helen Osborne, manager of Native Herb Products, in the herb garden
(Tilda Kemplen)

Tribes board meeting. Somebody had to drive. I couldn't, and Helen
thought she couldn't. So another staff member drove to Nashville.
But when we started back, we asked Helen to drive, and she said
she'd try. She drove all the way home. She said, "You know, if I'd
never gotten involved with all this and with Tilda to push and pull
me around and to get me to do these things, I never would have
gone to Nashville, and I never would have driven back." She was
really excited about that.

Not only has she grown up, but many other people, seeing that
Helen could do what she's done—become a manager of a big project
and supervisor of several people—have hope that they can do the
same thing or at least that they can make their talent in art work
for them. Before, they didn't know what to do with their talent, but

now they're using it by gathering their own materials to make beautiful products. It's really brought them out of a place of not knowing where to turn, to knowing that they can turn to their own abilities and look to themselves to make their own living.

For the past few years, I've been going to meetings and conferences on American Indian affairs to learn what benefits there were for them and what was going on. In the fall of 1987, I went to an Indian powwow down around Nashville along with six other people from around here, all of Cherokee heritage. It was the most beautiful celebration I've ever been to in my life, the most powerful, spiritual thing I've ever gone to. People from many, many different tribes came with their beautiful costumes, their dances, their singing, their stories—all to celebrate their heritage. The stories told by a man from Cherokee, North Carolina, were wonderful. He had heard them as a child growing up on the Cherokee reservation.

Iron Eyes Cody, the American Indian actor, was there. He offered an Indian prayer, and he offered a lot of encouragement to the Indian people. Close to the end of the ceremonies, he adopted a young woman from Georgia as his own daughter, and she adopted him as her own father. Iron Eyes Cody had begun to write his autobiography, and this woman was helping him with it and has been helping him with his work and writing for years. He expressed to the other Indian people his desire to adopt her as his own daughter, because his daughter had been killed in an accident. He wanted a daughter who could teach the things he had taught her. He gave her a brooch that had belonged to his mother and a collar of beads that had belonged to his wife. She gave him honey from Georgia and bread she had made. She vowed to learn of his teachings and his works and to teach others so that his teachings would never die. It was a very beautiful ceremony.

I appreciated so much what I saw there that day. All the people with me came home very encouraged and very excited about what the American Indians were doing and what we were trying to do, how we were trying to identify and learn to appreciate our heritage and our roots. It was so powerful and so spiritual that everybody seemed to have a real change in their lives and a real charge to go further. One of the things we want to do is have our group recognized as an American Indian group so that we too can participate in the conferences and the dances and whatever things are only for Indian people who are already recognized. We made a video recording of what happened at the powwow, and we brought it back and showed it to the rest of our staff and to our children and others in our communities. Everybody was really excited by it.

The American Indians were the first people in this country, and they highly valued the land and what it could produce. That is one of my main principles, loving the land, and taking care of and working it. The native people left us a great legacy, if we would follow it: to care for each other and care for the land. I would like to help people understand that and be proud to be Cherokee. Instead of just being Indian, they need to feel deeply within them that it's something they are able to be proud of and something they have to treasure and teach their children and their grandchildren.

I believe that our country has gone so far in the wrong direction of development that we need to get back to the basics. That's what the native people have taught us: how to live off the land, how to live with each other, the things that we can do for ourselves in the way of medicines and herbal cures for any illness—a simpler way of life. I think people are now trying to get back to that, but they don't know how. It's such a hard way for them to come back from the big city and big industry where they've been able to make a lot of money. They thought it helped them to be wealthier and have more material things, but the material things are now becoming less and less important to a lot of people. At the same time, it's frustrating, because they don't know how to get back to the basics.

One of the things we're trying to do in our ministry is to help people understand that you don't need much. You just need to care for what you have. You need to take care of your land and learn how to become familiar with the simple way of life. It could be the self-care you do, using the herbs and other things that grow to do some of the medical treatments we need instead of going to the doctor all the time and being killed with chemicals.

I learned about the trees, the flowers, and the herbs from my father and mother. My father learned it from his father who had been taught way back when he was young by an old Indian man called Indian Johnny. My grandfather delivered babies all over this area all during his life, until he was too old to walk over the mountains. He used herbal remedies on many things that ail people, because back then there were no doctors to go to, people just had to learn to be doctors themselves. Then my father followed that trade of doctoring, helping people with tonics and remedies that he could make, because he had learned it early in life by helping his father gather the herbs, barks, and roots for medicine. I would like to write a book on herbal and other home remedies from what I learned from my parents and grandparents.

I think there's a very close relationship between the Indians and mountain people. We learned to live by some of the ways the native people lived when there were lots of them in this part of the country. They showed the early pioneers which plants were edible and taught them how to track game and cultivate plants. Some of us keep and appreciate the simple life of farming the land, picking wild berries and nuts, and preserving our food by methods like drying. I feel a strong kinship with Indian people. I love their way of life much more than the so-called white man's way.

I've never been able to fit into the society that has to have fancy clothes and fancy houses. I love the basic, simple things. At heart I am Indian, and I love the Indian people. Everywhere I go I talk about them, and I would love to be more involved with the things they do now. American Indians are trying to help other people recognize what they do, what they've done, and what they stand for; it's beautiful. I feel that the American Indians try to live the way God planned for us to live, on what He created, not what we create—and destroy.

One way we have tried to strengthen our connection to the land is through the Mountain Communities Small Farms Program. This program evolved to try to address both the high unemployment rate and people's lack of skill in raising livestock, gardening, and preserving food in our communities. The intent is to assist families in raising livestock and growing food in limited space. This program has grown out of our experience with the Mountain Communities Livestock Project and our small projects in gardening and greenhouse operation and management. With seeds from Keep America Beautiful and support from two church organizations (the Board for Social Ministry Services of the Lutheran Church Missouri Synod and the Presiding Bishop's Fund for World Relief, the relief arm of the Episcopal Church), we began the initial planning and coordination in October 1989, with hope of finding ongoing funding.

The program helps families grow their own food so that they are less dependent on society for all their needs and so they can survive where they are, where they want to be. It instills a sense of self-esteem and self-worth and helps people become self-reliant, instead of dependent on emergency food distribution, food stamps, welfare, or any other source of survival assistance. We also want to help improve families' nutrition. Hunger and poor nutrition are some of the root causes of poor health, which contributes to low self-esteem, poor motivation, and ongoing poverty.

We knew there was a need for this program, since our organization has received many requests for emergency food. Many of the recipient families have shown an interest in growing their own food, sometimes with new methods of gardening. They have also shown interest in learning how to preserve food. We help the unemployed, underemployed, handicapped, disabled, elderly, children, and other community people who live at or below the poverty level. Around a hundred to two hundred families are helped by the small farms program each year.

We know what people can do for themselves if they are given the opportunity. This program helps the community learn a new method of gardening by providing materials, supplies, and equipment to get started, as well as technical assistance and training. Workshops include greenhouse operation, the French intensive gardening method, plant choice, planting, growing, and record keeping. People are also taught food preservation, including canning, freezing, and drying, so they'll have good food during the winter months.

We train people mainly through a demonstration farm located on property owned by our organization. It is bottom land with a nearby creek. We have access to city water hook-up for irrigation if necessary. We demonstrate how to grow more food in limited space, using the French intensive gardening method. This method uses double-dug, raised beds, four feet wide by eight feet long, so the plants are easy to care for by one person standing on either side. Vegetables, herbs, and flowers are grown organically, without the use of chemical sprays and fertilizers. There are also small fruit trees on the demonstration farm, which bear apples, pears, and peaches.

The gardening ties in with the greenhouse and livestock operations. The greenhouse provides plants, and cows supply natural fertilizer. So we're able to train people how to fit raising livestock in with gardening.

Community members are involved by doing the actual work on the demonstration farm and by learning methods to apply to run their own small family farms. We provide them with seeds and plants at little or no cost. People can sell the produce they don't use themselves at farmers' markets. They can also barter for needed items with other community members. As well as being grown and distributed to the demonstration garden and gardens in the communities, greenhouse plants are being sold to outside businesses and agencies. Plans include a seed bank and the development of a local farmers market. We hope to see people planting and marketing pick-your-own strawberries, blackberries, raspberries, and blueberries. Helping people run their own small family farms encourages them to become more self-sufficient. We want families to be able to stay on the land and in the place they love and call home.

Three

My Personal Life

DEALING WITH ILLNESS

During my working years, I've had to deal with several major illnesses. It seems that I have only rare diseases that are hard to diagnose and treat. The ones I've had that have really gotten me down—histoplasmosis, aplastic anemia, and Legionnaires' disease—are diseases not too many people have.

I was teaching at Fonde Elementary School in Fonde, Kentucky, when I had histoplasmosis. The doctors explained that it was like a little fuzzy mold on your lungs that secretes a lot of fluid and causes you to cough and cough until you are so weak and nervous you can hardly stand it. I had never been very sick, but this time I was. I had to be on sick leave for six months under a doctor's care, in and out of the hospital. It was hard to deal with and to overcome, but I got over it.

One of the things that helped me was reading a book about John Wesley (the founder of Methodism) that talked about his having had tuberculosis as a young man. It described a method he used to help him get through his illness, which was coughing one less cough each time he started. I tried that, because nothing else was working.

I believed that if it could help John Wesley, it could help me too. It did help. As you cough one less time, that's one less irritation to the bronchial tubes and lungs.

The next illness I got was aplastic anemia. I didn't know what was going on. I just got tired, and I got to where I couldn't function well. I thought I was working too hard. I couldn't stay awake a lot of times. When I got really sick at my stomach and my head hurt, I went to the doctor. He thought I just had low blood. He gave me some iron pills and told me to take those for a week and come back. The next day or two I was getting worse, sick at my stomach and vomiting.

I called the doctor and asked if those pills would make me sick. He said they shouldn't. I went back to the clinic, and he drew my blood again. It was even lower than before I'd started taking the iron pills. He asked if somebody could take me to the hospital, because I needed to have some blood. I went to Jellico Hospital, and that was the beginning of my blood transfusions. They knew they had to give me blood to keep me alive, but they didn't know the cause of my condition.

The first thing they thought of was cancer, so they started testing me for it. They put me through every test there is to be put through, I guess, and through every scan there is to be done and never found any cancer anywhere. They couldn't believe that I was losing blood without it going somewhere, and they couldn't find where it was going. Dr. Jessie Lee Walker tried to do a bone marrow test on me at Jellico Hospital after they'd done all the other tests; that was the last one they were going to do. He couldn't find any bone marrow. So he got me an appointment with Dr. Alan Solomon, the hematologist at Baptist Hospital in Knoxville, and sent me there. I stayed there and went through all their tests, all their lab work and everything. They couldn't figure out what was going on. They did several bone marrow tests and couldn't find any bone marrow either.

Dr. Solomon asked if I would go to the National Heart, Lung, and Blood Institute of the National Institutes of Health in Bethesda,

Maryland, if he could get me an appointment. He told me that if there was any place in the world that could diagnose what was going on, it was there. I told him I'd go anywhere, because my condition was going downhill fast without any blood. I was having to take blood transfusions often. You don't feel too good when you have to take blood. I was taking four units every week or two. Finally the platelets in my blood got so low that I was bleeding out of my nose and my mouth. That's when I went to the National Heart, Lung, and Blood Institute.

They had already diagnosed my case as aplastic anemia, which means the bone marrow doesn't make blood cells any longer. They asked me to take an experimental treatment that would take twenty-one days. I told them I couldn't stay there that long, because my husband was too sick. They put it off, and I put it off. Finally it got to the point where my blood count was really low. The doctor told me that my platelet count was two thousand and that it's supposed to be two hundred thousand. Platelets only live for one day. I'd take ten units of platelets one day, and I'd have to take them again the next day. I was so weak I could hardly walk. I almost lost my memory and all my thinking and writing power. Without blood flowing to your brain, you don't have much to work with. I had so little blood that it was almost as if my whole body was being destroyed. Without plate-lets, blood won't clot. Every time I'd blow my nose and every time I'd cough, there would be blood. I was bleeding constantly. That's when I agreed to take the experimental treatment.

As part of the treatment, they used an intravenous serum made from rattlesnake venom implanted in live horseflesh. I was the hundredth person who had ever taken it. When I signed myself into the hospital to take the treatment in 1982, they told me about all the side effects it could have. They told me that I could die from the shock. The doctors asked if any members of my family were there to sign my papers. I told them that I didn't want my family to sign my papers and that I would sign them.

The physician's assistant at the local clinic sent me to Jellico Hospital. From there, I went to Baptist Hospital, and from there I went to the National Heart, Lung, and Blood Institute. I did what the doctors told me to do, and if they asked me to go further, to another doctor, I never made excuses. I didn't say, "I can't," or "I don't want to." I went every step with them, because I believed that they were the best doctors in the world and that they were doing the right thing.

At the same time that I was following their directions, I took notice of what I had to do. I realized they could only do so much, that this was my body, and I had to take care of it, too. Instead of just taking the chemicals they had to give me and not eating well, I tried to eat right. I didn't even like food then, because while taking the steroids I gained a lot of weight. They made me really heavy and made me want to eat whether I needed to or not. I didn't like that. Steroids were destroying my whole system, and I hated taking them. But I had hope I was getting better, and I took them for blood building purposes.

The doctor had told me what the steroids were made of and how dangerous they were. He wanted to help me get off them when I no longer needed them. It took three or four trials, because every time I'd quit taking them, my blood count would begin going back down, and he'd say, "We've just got to try them again." Then they'd give me a smaller dose and try to keep me on enough to keep my blood building. The steroids were so powerful that the doctor said if I went off them all at one time, I could go into shock and die. By tapering off really slowly, my blood became normal, for me anyway.

I've gone through many terrible withdrawals, trying to get my body to function instead of the medicines creating the energy for my body to work. But I've never yet given in to taking any more of the steroids, no matter how sick I've gotten by not having them, and I'm really proud of that. That wasn't a struggle for me, because I set myself the goal that I would not take them unless my blood got down so low that I would have to. I got some good vitamins, and I started replenishing my body with vitamins that the steroids were destroying. Even when I was still in the hospital, I asked my friend, Lou Malicoat, to brew up and send me a quart of goldenseal herb tea; it's a real healer. I think that helped me to get well, taking things into my body to try to counteract what they had to give me to take in. I believed it would help, so it did.

I'd lost almost all use of my body. My legs were getting in really bad shape. I couldn't walk more than out to the driveway. When I had no strength to keep going, it was hard to try, but I did. I had a treadle sewing machine, and I don't know how, but I got it out to the kitchen. I used it to build up the muscles in my legs, because I could sit and treadle over and over; it was like riding a bicycle. That helped me get back enough strength in my legs to start walking. I was taking the vitamins, doing my exercises, and doing everything I could for myself. Nobody told me; nobody suggested these things. I just realized what I had to do to help myself and to help the doctors, because if I didn't take care of myself, they couldn't take care of me—they could when I was in the hospital, but they couldn't when I was out.

I spent a great deal of time in hospitals. I couldn't take regular blood plasma; I had to take the wash cells. That meant they took out everything that could cause any allergic reaction. For a long time, I had to go all the way to Knoxville every day to have some test or to let them draw blood so that they could see what was going on. Then it got to be every week, and I went every week for a long, long time. I took many treatments of chemotherapy. As I began to get better, I could go every two weeks. I went that way for a long time. When the doctor saw that things were continuing to stay pretty stable, he let me come each month, and I went every month for a long, long time. Now I go to the same doctor every six months. He needs to keep up with my progress. If my blood count began to get low, I'd need him.

Something I learned from being sick was patience. When I first knew that I was sick—not just tired and needing rest—my mind and my system wouldn't allow that. So I had to work on it really hard for a long time, to make myself lie down and rest so that I wouldn't be so tired and so my body could heal. That was a real experience for me, too, trying to learn to rest. I had never needed to rest before, because I had all the energy I needed, and I could go on and on and on. When my blood got so low, that energy was gone. My body would say, "Rest," and my mind would say, "Go." So I was in a terrible position there for a while, battling to do both, trying to hold together my body, soul, and mind and make them all work together. It was so hard, but I finally got through it.

I really don't want to rest now. Ever since I got well, I have felt an urge to work harder, because my vision keeps getting bigger and bigger, and my goal gets further and further away. I hope I never get to where I can't keep working on something. It's hard sometimes to keep on going when I don't feel well, and there are times when I don't.

I had a near-death experience when I had aplastic anemia. By the tenth day of the experimental treatment, I was really sick. My skin was about one-quarter inch thick. The rash was terrible. I had so much pain in my body, I could hardly stand it. I didn't have enough blood to keep me going. I ached all the time. They'd give me medicines, but nothing stopped the pain. It was so hard to live.

My family had come to the hospital, but I sent them home, because I didn't want them to see me that sick. I didn't know if I was going to die or what was going to happen, but I didn't want my daughter, Chris, or my daughter-in-law, Betty, to be there. I walked the floor all night. All night long I prayed for the Lord to have his way. Whatever He did would be all right with me.

In my mind was the book of Job, where the Lord asked Satan, "Hast thou considered my servant Job?"

Satan answered the Lord, "Hast not Thou made a hedge about him?"

Job had always been my favorite scripture, and I'd read it a lot of times. I liked the patience and the kindness that he showed. That's the only scripture that came to my mind; it just flowed all night long. I knew that I was hedged in.

I saw some big hands that I thought were the big hands of God, and the whole world was in them. I was in there; I was in those hands. Then I went into a deep sleep. I don't know how long I was asleep or how long I was in this valley of the shadow of death. I saw myself in bed, and up above me stood an angel. She spoke to me and said, "I'm the angel of mercy."

While she was standing above me, what I believe to be the "Great Physician," our Lord, with white hair and white coat, was sitting beside my bed, with his back to me. I only saw the back of his head. I don't believe anyone has ever been able to look upon his face. He was big. His arm was on my bed, protecting me with his great power. I don't know how long I was in this valley, but I knew He was protecting me, and I knew that the scripture that had been running through my mind was telling me that He was protecting me, that He had my life hedged in.

When I came out of the valley and was awake again, I called the nurse. When she came, I asked, "Do you have an angel of mercy working here?" It scared her so badly that she jerked the rails up around my bed and ran for the doctor. My room was really close to the nurses' desk because they were expecting all kinds of things to happen with that treatment. They knew that I was really sick. I guess they thought I was going to die.

The doctor ran in and said, "Where's her family?"

I said, "I sent them home."

He said, "Get the intensive care unit ready," and the nurse went to get it ready. The doctor started drawing out my blood.

I begged, "Please don't take my blood."

The doctor said, "I have to." He was sitting on the side of my bed.

I begged, "Please don't. I'm turned around. I'm going to get well. You know I don't have much blood anyway, so don't draw it out."

They thought I was dying. I'm sure they needed that blood for medical research purposes. But I kept asking the doctor not to draw any more blood, and he finally stopped.

I said, "Will you promise me that I won't have to take any more treatment? I'm turned around, and I'm going to get well." That's all that was in my mind: "I'm turned around, and I'm going to get well." He said they wouldn't give me any more medicines or other treatment.

The woman doctor who came to see me the next morning said, "Boy, you gave everybody a scare last night."

I said, "What did I do?"

She said, "It was the stories you told."

And I said, "But I didn't tell any stories. I told the real truth. That's really what happened to me."

She said, "But you scared people with it, because they thought you were gone."

I said: "No. I was coming back; I was on my way back."

She said: "I think you really did go into death, because we've had many experiences with that, but never one just like yours. We've had people who have had similar experiences as they went into death."

I went to sleep and slept like a baby for two weeks, except when they'd wake me up to give me something to drink. My mouth was in such bad shape I could hardly drink. But for two weeks I was under that healing power of the Great Physician, with not a pain in my body. I had come back from whatever stage of death or life I had been in. And in two weeks' time, I was much better. In a month, I was ready to come home.

That was an experience that let me know that I had greater things to do and that the Lord would always be with me and would never leave me. Even through death, I would not be alone. That's why I don't have to worry about the great beyond. I live my life so that I don't have to worry about what's on the other side. I know it will be something beautiful, peaceful, and wonderful. When people have been interviewed about their premonitions of death, a lot of them have said that they experienced really bad things, that they saw hell and fire. I didn't experience anything bad. I experienced only good things. It was such a beautiful experience that I have had no fear of death since that time.

One time a social work professor at the University of Tennessee, Dr. Paul Zarbock, called Marie Cirrillo, a mutual friend. When she heard Paul's voice, Marie said, "Well, the dead has come to life," as you might say if you hadn't heard from someone for a long time.

And he said, "That's true, Marie."

She said, "What do you mean?"

He said, "Really, I did experience death."

She said, "You know, Tilda had a similar experience."

He said, "Call her and ask if I can come up there so we can share our experiences with each other."

Very soon after that he brought some students and came up to see me. This big, big guy put his arms around me and cried. Then he told me about his experience and asked me to share mine with him and his students. Because of his experience, he wanted his students to hear about mine. When they've had similar experiences, it's good for people to share them. He didn't experience anything bad either, so we had similar stories to tell.

It became apparent that I was coming down with all these strange, rare illnesses, and so many of my neighbors were dying from cancer and blood diseases. It came to me that we live in an environment with lots of problems and that there has to be an environmental factor behind our illnesses. We live and work in an area where there are open strip mining pits, abandoned deep mines, schools filled with asbestos materials, dusty roads, and polluted streams. Not only do our own people destroy us with their efforts to become wealthy and powerful, but the rest of the nation looks upon Appalachia as a dumping ground for hazardous waste products. Abandoned strip mining ponds are looked at as perfect dumping places. I'm sure that all this is connected with the high rate of lung cancer, black lung disease, leukemia, and other blood diseases like aplastic anemia, the form of bone marrow cancer that took me into the valley of death. The Lord brought me out and gave me the strength and courage to write this book and do many other things.

During the time I was sick with anemia, I developed glaucoma and cataracts both at the same time, and from the way my eyes were failing, I thought that I was surely going to lose my sight. I began to think about all the beautiful things that I had seen down through the years: children's faces; my mother, father, brother, sisters, and husband; my babies when they were born; my grandchildren, aunts, uncles, nieces, nephews, and cousins; friends and neighbors, teachers, classmates, and other people; my church, the Bible, and songs; rivers, streams, meadows, rocks, hills, and mountains; trees, flowers, and seeds; birds, fish, bees, and butterflies. I was conditioning myself to become blind, and I had all those pictures in my mind. I knew I had enough beauty to last me throughout whatever life I had left to live. I knew I could handle being blind. It would have been hard for me to get around and do my work, but I think I would have continued. As it turned out, I had cataract surgery, and the doctors treated the glaucoma.

After recovering from the dread disease of aplastic anemia, I did quite well for about five years. Then on April 16, 1989, I was struck down with another rare and terrible illness called Legionnaires' disease. I stayed in the hospital twelve days and at home in bed for another three weeks. I am still trying to overcome it. I am again climbing that great, high mountain of getting well. I am so thankful that I can tell the story about having the disease. I've not seen or heard of many who have survived it. In May 1989, we heard of two deaths from Legionnaires' disease, one in Knoxville and one in Pennington Gap, Virginia.

My experience when I was sick with Legionnaires' disease was quite different from my near-death experience during my illness with aplastic anemia. While I was in the hospital, it seems that I was "out-of-body," making journeys, trying to do all the things that had been on my mind to do before I fell ill. In my first out-of-body experience, I was trying to get home to make out my will and help the children know which of my material possessions I wanted each one to have. I accomplished this. I told my children and grandchildren that I had very little to leave them except what I believe in, what I stand for, principles to live by, and my love for them.

Before I fell ill, my family, friends, and staff bought rosebushes for my sixty-fourth birthday on March 23 for me to plant in my garden. In my vision, I was trying to get home to plant my rose garden. I traveled some bad, rough roads, and all along the way I could see large rosebushes that people had dug up and thrown away. That disturbed me, because I wanted so badly to get mine planted. But I never found my way home.

In my next experience, I was at a cemetery at my own funeral. I was looking up at the tent that was over the grave. People were sitting around under the tent. Then I saw a beautiful, well-dressed lady come around the corner of the tent. When she got to where she could see me, she looked down at me and smiled. Then it seemed that everything was okay.

The thing that helped me most to keep going through my illnesses and all the treatments was having the revelation that I was going to get well. I wanted to get well, because I had lots of things I wanted to do. I could see the need for doing many things that anybody could have done if they had decided to. But I didn't think anybody else would do some of the things I wanted to see done. One of the things I wanted to do was to leave this history of what I've experienced in my life and my work. I think maybe that helped me to keep the faith and helped me to believe that I was getting well. Without that faith, I don't think I would have made it, because if you don't have faith and hope, you don't even try. I wanted to help my children and my grandchildren to have simple, happy lives. They probably could have done it without me, but I've always prayed for God to let me raise my children and help raise my grandchildren. Each day I see the fruits of my labors and enjoy my family and friends, and I thank God for helping me through all my trials.

I believe there is a Heaven, but I have never dwelled on the fact that I want to do good on this earth so I can go to Heaven. I want to do good on this earth because I want to help people. There's a Heaven, and I'm bound for it; that's fine. But I would like to make a little bit of Heaven on this earth with my own views and vision and with some of the things that I can do. Never have I had a vision of being in Heaven. My vision has been just doing the best I can from day to day. Whatever God has beyond earth, I don't know; that's his plan, that's his work. If we can relieve some of the suffering in this world, I think that's what we need to be trying to do.

What I really want to leave my children and my grandchildren, and my friends and neighbors, is what I stand for and what I have done. Maybe I've not done anything so great, but I want to leave behind the things I've done that they can remember and appreciate. I want to pass on my love for people and the way we show our care for each other. I also want to pass on my love for the land and what it can produce. That's all I'll have, because I won't have any money. The important things are my beliefs and the principles and standards I live by; that's what I want to leave with them. I want them to always remember the values I have about life and people and how my life influenced their lives.

I don't want to keep anything I appreciate a lot. I want to give it away. I want to share it. If people can just remember me for being the person who didn't want to keep things. You don't have any love until you've given it all away. You don't have anything until you've given it all away. That's what I'd like to pass on. I'd like my children and grandchildren somehow to step in and follow after and not ever become selfish with each other or with other people.

I know that my whole life is held in the hands of God, and I don't have to be afraid. It is love that motivates me, not fear. But if I have a fear, it is of doing anything I know is really wrong or bad. If I knowingly went against what I stand for and what I know is right, I'd be afraid that the Lord would not be pleased and that I would have to pay for that. I'd be afraid to turn my back on my beliefs and step off my principles for my own selfish reasons. I guess that's not really a fear, because I don't worry about it, and I'm not going to as long as my mind is working so I can keep control of what I do. If I'm ever out of control, I wouldn't be held responsible anyway.

I have a hard time with people who always worry about getting old and with people who don't want to get over thirty. I say, "Just wait until you're sixty," because I feel that over the past few years I've become so much more alert and so much more able to do the things I've wanted than I've ever been in my life. I've had more opportunities to go places and do things I've realized a need for. I've been involved with many people, churches, and government agencies and have been able to learn more. I don't think my age keeps me from doing anything I want to do.

I don't mind aging. I know it's a part of the plan of life. I don't ever want to be unable to take care of myself, but if that happens to fall to my lot, I'll have to deal with it. I have the advantage of having my children and grandchildren around. It's been a great strength for me to see them take an interest in the ministry to which I have dedicated my life and to know they will carry on my work. The only things I've ever really asked God for were patience, strength, faith, love, knowledge, and wisdom. These are the things I value most, because these are the things that help me do what I see as my lot.

MY RELATIONSHIPS AND MY HOME

At the age of sixteen, I met and fell in love with James Kemplen, the man I wanted to spend my life with, but my parents were totally against my dating him. Church was the only place

Tilda's husband, James Kemplen

young people could go. We had to walk about three miles to church, so that was the way we got to see each other. We dated for almost three years. Then we slipped off and went to the nearest town, which was twenty miles away, to get a blood test at a hospital. We went to pick up the results after a three-day wait and went to a justice of the peace. We were married on April 1, April Fools' Day. We always joked about who got fooled.

When I got married and took those vows, to me it meant that I had to be true to those vows and live them out. Even though it was not always easy, it was something I had to do to be true to what I'd said to myself and to my husband, and to my family and to God. I was very dedicated and sincere about my vows, and I did the best I knew how. We both stuck to our commitment to each other and made it work. Our marriage lasted thirty-nine years, with no separation or divorce.

When nearly everyone left the area to find jobs, we just stayed here and did the best we could and had a pretty good life together. We had a hard time making a living, because Jim was a coal miner, and this was the time when deep mining was winding down and jobs were almost a thing of the past. Jim worked in small truck mines, sawmills, or wherever he could. Both of us knew how to farm and garden, so we raised a lot of our food. This helped us to be able to stay in the area. Jim was a good husband and father. I was a good wife and mother. This does not mean that life was an easy street or a bed of roses. We had our ups and downs and hard times, as with most couples.

About a year after we were married, we had a son. He was named James Elijah II. He died from a heart condition when he was two days old. Two and a half years later, I had another child, Ralph. Two and a half years after that, I had my daughter, Chris. It just happened that the births were spaced out that way; I didn't know how to plan them. It was kind of neat having both my children little at the same time. It was hard, but it was good too because we all grew up together. I always thought it was better to have them together than it was to have one and someday have another one. Older people always give you advice on how to do everything, and I did get help from Mother. But mostly I just did what I thought was all right about being a wife and mother. I did the best I knew how.

I raised not only my own two children, but a niece and two nephews stayed with me more than they stayed anywhere else, because their mother and daddy had separated. Jim was very good at helping me with the children. I couldn't have made it so well otherwise. When my daughter, Chris, was born, he took complete care of our son, Ralph. Jim was good to my nieces and nephews, and I was good to his. We always had some of them around. Our house and yard were always full of children.

It was hard for me then, sharing my life with so many children, helping them all in any way I could and trying to make ends meet. But now it's really great to have that other family, an extended family.

I have my children and grandchildren here and my niece and two nephews and their families living in Georgia and Chicago. It's like having another set of children and another set of grandchildren.

I'd been very sick with aplastic anemia for a couple of years when Jim got really sick. But we still struggled along and did whatever we could to help each other. His death from the miner's disease, black lung, and a related heart disease in 1982 was a shock to me, but I didn't grieve. People ask me if I wear black because I'm in mourning over my husband's death. I tell them I never mourned, because I felt that we'd had a pretty full life, and I had fulfilled my promises and my vows. His death was hard on me, but I never stopped doing what I was doing. I just went on with my life.

I've always stayed on a pretty even keel throughout losing my father and mother, a child, and a husband. I've never stopped and sat down and grieved. I've tried to go forward instead of looking backward. I've just kept on working and have never stopped just because there was an obstacle in the way or something came up that could have thrown me off track. I have just stuck right with what I believe in and done the best I could to make things work.

I have two grown children who live next to me. I had a very good relationship with my children as they grew up. I always respected them and their views, and they respected both Jim and me as their parents. They both quit high school during their final year. They had to go away from home to find jobs. As soon as they found a way, they both came back home to live. They wanted to live here, just as most people want to come back home when they leave here. It's been really good to have them around. During our illnesses, we had two children who were close by and could help us through it all.

We still have a good relationship. I go my way and do my things. They're supportive of what I do, and I'm supportive of what they do. We counsel with each other once in a while about being careful, saying, "Don't get sick," that kind of thing. But nobody tells anybody else what to do. We understand each other. We share almost everything we have. If one needs whatever the other one's got, it is shared.

I have watched my children mature. They're both in their forties now. Young people come through long, hard years of trying to raise a young family, and yet I've seen them become very involved and very caring about the things that I have cared so much about.

My daughter, Chris McKillop, works closely with me. The reason she came back home was that I got sick and was not able to function very well to keep the administration going for the child care program. She saw that, and she knew how much I loved what I was doing and how strongly I felt about it. She came home and began to learn how to make it work. If it hadn't been for her, things wouldn't be nearly as far along as they are, because she just took over the administrative part of the work. She's still doing that, because as I got better, I began more projects and didn't have time to go back to the bookkeeping and the administrative part of the programs. She learned from scratch, on her own, how to manage all that.

After getting her GED, she went on to college. She has completed almost three years of course work in administration. It's been hard for her to find time to finish the work for her degree, because she has been the head of her household and the only breadwinner in the family. She has two children at home, Brenden and Daniel (we call him "Bucky"). Her daughter, Jami, my oldest granddaughter, stays with me.

My son, Ralph, worked three years at the pallet factory and did a lot of the managing there while it was in operation. He works in the livestock project. As one of the board members who helps make decisions, he's one of the people who has been very instrumental in making it work. He and a lot of other men have taken this project and are making it a success.

For a while he did well with his hog business. When he no longer could make money at that, he sold his hogs and bought a log truck and developed his own timber-cutting and logging job. Ralph's wife,

Tilda's son, Ralph Kemplen, with his wife, Betty, and their two children, Tammy and James (Nancy Herzberg)

Tilda and the McKillop family: daughter Chris (kneeling) and grandchildren (from left) Brenden, Jami, and Daniel (Nancy Herzberg)

Betty, works as a cook at the day care center. They have two children, Tammy and James. Ralph has another son, Michael, who lives in Ohio.

I like it when Ralph and his friends come and sit around my table. It's like having a council meeting; they come here for support. They like to come here to talk about things they're not sure of and ask how I would handle something. I always try to let them understand that you don't have to fight over anything, that you don't have to get angry when certain things happen. I get angry sometimes, but it's because I let myself. I try to instill in them the good that can come when they keep from getting mad and saying things that will hurt somebody or that they'll have to feel guilty about.

I'm told that as a grandparent I've played the role of spoiling my grandchildren. What I've tried to do with them is the same thing I've tried to do with my children and with other children I've come in contact with—love and care for them and make them feel good. I always want them to feel that whatever I have is theirs. They can walk in my door any time they want to and take anything they want from my refrigerator.

I think the children feel good about being here, and I feel good that they're here close to me. I know what it was like when Chris was away with her children. I was always going to New York City to see them, because they were my first grandchildren. Now my grandchildren look out for me, too. They do a great many things, like helping stack my wood and finding out if I'm all right. Even the youngest one, James, comes to my house two or three times a day just to ask, "Are you all right?" or "What are you doing?" It's really important to me.

My neighbors and other friends I've made are a real support system for me. Some of the people I care the most about and who have been closest to me through the years are people I can really talk with. They're always wanting to know where I am and what I'm doing. They want to know that I'm all right. I'm the same way with them, but I don't show it as much as they do. I don't need to keep up with people as much as some people need to keep up with me. They really appreciate the way I've conducted my life. They're supportive of all the things I'm doing. There aren't many people out trying to create jobs and make schools and projects work.

Many of the most supportive people are women I've helped with jobs or other things, or whose children I've helped. If people know you care about their children, it makes them supportive of whatever you do. When Governor Ned McWherter came to our child care center, one woman had tears in her eyes as she told the governor about how I took care of the children, how I worked with them, and how much they appreciated my being their teacher. I didn't realize people felt that way until that day. So I do have a great support system through mothers.

A lot of men are also very supportive of what I do. Some are intimidated by me, but you can expect that. Men have been the ones who had jobs throughout the years, for as long as I can remember. In the past, women didn't have jobs. The men have a greater appreciation now than they did a few years ago for a woman who can come up out of a community like ours and go out and make things happen, like offering jobs not only to women but to men.

I have many special friends from outside the area, including people from various church organizations that have supported our work. My circle of friends keeps widening. Vimala Nataraj is a courageous woman from India who came to our community through a grass-roots leadership exchange. After returning to India, Vim decided that she wanted to come back to our community, because she liked what she saw taking place in our organization. She corresponded with me about the possibility of coming for another visit, and we agreed that she should. She stayed with me for some time and fit into the education and teaching part of our work perfectly. We sponsored her application for an extended visa. This was approved and allowed her to bring her husband and daughter to the United States.

I'm not at all interested in dating. I like all kinds of people, and I like having friends, both men and women. I've had some very good, very true men friends, and I have good relationships with them, talking, working, going places. They appreciate me for who I am, and I appreciate them for who they are, and we let it go that way. We're good friends, and that's it. Remarriage is not on my list at all. I'm too busy. No man would want to try to keep up with me; I don't know one who would. I'm totally happy with my life, very satisfied.

I couldn't do the things I do if I had to stop and explain to somebody what I'm doing all the time. I wouldn't get to do anything. I'd always be explaining. I don't want any ties. I want to come home and sit at my kitchen table if I want to. I want to go to bed if I want to. Then if I want to get up and go somewhere, I'll get up and go. I don't have to tell anybody that I'm going or when I'll be back. I can make split-second decisions without any problem, because I don't have to ask anybody anything, and I'm in complete control of what I try to do and want to do.

I really don't feel lonely too much because there's always so much to do that there's little time to feel lonely. The only time I feel lonely is possibly on Saturdays and Sundays when the work week is kind of finished, and I come home and wish there were something yet to do. A lot of times there is, because most of the time my phone is ringing all day and night, and people are coming to see me, wanting jobs and all kinds of things. When I do get to feeling lonely, I go over and talk with someone or have supper with them. I stay high as a kite most of the time, because these are the kinds of things that make me function well. I need a lot in my life to make me happy, and I've got it. Even in the autumn, when a lot of people say, "I just can't stand this time of year when the leaves are falling," to me it's just a great, beautiful time. I don't get sad and feel all out of sorts too much. The only time is when I'm sick, and I try to sleep that off and not let it bother me.

I've walked through the woods all my life, and at times when I'm not really busy I like to get out and just go and see all the beauty that's out there. I like to gather things and bring them in for others to enjoy, like Indian arrow-wood, one of the most beautiful of all the shrubbery growing wild. There are no flower gardens anywhere more beautiful than what's out in the woods growing wild. I've always been fascinated by what comes out of the ground. When I go into the mountains, it's a sacred place I go to. The farther back in the mountains I go, the better I feel. When I get into a real mountain setting on back in the mountains where I grew up, it seems to me that I'm in a great cathedral that God has given us, with wildflowers on green moss for a carpet, the sky for a ceiling, and the trees filled with colorful leaves and birds. Buildings don't do that for me, but the open spaces of the mountains do.

I feel very strongly that the mountains are shelter to me; they are a shield. I feel very safe here, and when I look at a mountain, it seems like my refuge. I always think of the scripture, "I will lift up mine eyes unto the hills." Every time I go away from here, when I come back and start to see these hills rising up, that's what I think of. With that good feeling within me, I want to go places and do things, but I want to come back. When I go to certain places like the school or the church where I went as a child, I feel as if I'm walking on sacred ground, because these are such holy places to me. This is where my heart is, and this is where I want to be.

By being out in the woods, I've learned a lot about nature and how and why I appreciate it so much. First of all, I believe and have faith in God, and nature is his glorious creation. I have great love for all of God's creation, and I feel part of it all. I know that I had a really good start in learning to appreciate the natural beauty of life by following around after my father, going fishing and hunting. I also worked the garden and took walks with my mother and my aunt, Laura Kempton. I went with them to pick blackberries and hunt for hickory nuts, walnuts, and hazelnuts. We lived really close to the woods, and it always just fascinated me to go beyond the cleared places, like pasture land, and see the woods outside. It's tranquil and nerve-soothing. The nature I see is a great part of my life. Sometimes I stop on the roadside or hillsides to get a picture with my camera, and many times poetry fills my mind.

The woods are where our love of nature first takes root. It's a habitat you just can't get away from. There's something about the woods, the mountains, the streams, the flowers, the birds, the trees, the whole of nature. It encourages me and gives me strength to see such beauty. I wonder how many people see the beauty around them every day, and how many people in this world have no beauty around them. All I need when I'm down and out is just to walk out the road, walk in the woods, along a mountain stream, and listen to the birds and other wonderful sounds.

It's very important to me to be here. I think that same love of nature is being instilled in my children and their children. I like to think I've helped a lot of other people, especially the children I've been able to teach, to love the things close by that God created for them: paths, nature walks, flowers, and trees.

Many people have left the area to find jobs. Some might say they don't want to come back, but almost all the people I know who have left these mountains feel a drawing power from them, especially as they grow older. They want to come back and retire here. They want to come back to the farms, even though the farms are small. People really do appreciate what they have a part in producing or creating. It's a way of life. People who live in these mountains have a deep love for them and their beauty.

I've talked a lot about a root system, how people are rooted in their heritage and in their culture. That root system spreads through the love we have for one another and the appreciation we have for our homes and the mountains. I put down roots early in life. It means a lot to me to be able to stay here in these beautiful mountains where I was born and raised and where I am in constant contact with my family. I've got my immediate family living next to me, and most of the rest of my family, like my sister and her daughter, live nearby.

Land doesn't really belong to anyone, only to God who created it for our use and enjoyment. Land and people all belong to the Great Landlord who created us all. But it's been really important to me to own some land and to own my own home. I grew up in whatever house my family could rent. We put down roots wherever we were. Only after I had children of my own were my husband and I able to buy the land that my children and I now have our homes on. We've been able to anchor our roots and have a place to really call home. I'd have a hard time living in somebody else's house. I don't want other people telling me what I can and cannot do.

I want to emphasize the importance of owning a home, of having a piece of land you can call your own where your children and grand-children can be around you. It's important that they can go out and do whatever they need to, because they are in control of that little piece of land. They can build a house or pitch a tent, whatever makes them happy. It's a unique family circle we all appreciate so much.

My husband, Jim, and I lived in Guy Hollow for a while. When the kids were small, we built a house right down the hill from where I now live. In 1956, when our children were school age, we bought ten acres of land from the Methodist Church. They had built the Archer Center School on it (they eventually closed that school). We converted the Methodist parsonage to our house and lived there from 1956 until 1985. We also had land we could farm or use for pasture. We could do whatever we needed to do, whatever seemed important. The land was used for recreational purposes several summers, because our community had no recreational facilities. When our children got married and wanted to come home, they had a place where they could build houses. It meant everything to us to have a home of our own that we had worked to pay for and were able to do with whatever we wanted.

My home was destroyed by a wood stove fire following a Christmas Day dinner in 1985. The fire began in an attic flue. Most of my dinner guests left shortly before the fire broke out around the chim-

Tilda in front of her home (Warren Brunner)

ney. I managed to save some important papers and family photo-graphs. Two of my neighbors made several dashes inside my burning home and managed to get out some of my furniture. My precious quilts, quilt tops, and pillows were destroyed. I lost practically every-thing I owned. When my house burned down, it was the loneliest feeling I ever had. I didn't have anywhere to call home after all the years of having one. I just had to watch it all burn down, and there was nothing I could do about it.

My brother had lived in our house since my husband died. He didn't have a home of his own. He had separated from his family years ago and came here to live. Although he wasn't well, he helped me support our home, and I appreciated just knowing he was here and having somebody to cook for and have around. My cousin's husband, a cancer patient, also lived with us. I rented a house because of them, so that they could have a home and it wouldn't be too hard for them. I went and bought a stove and got just a few things together. Two days after the house burned, my brother fell sick with a severe stroke, and that took my mind off the house during the remaining time he lived, a little over a month. During his illness, I spent almost all my time at the hospital with him. The year 1985, when my house burned down and my brother got sick, was a very hard time for me.

I took a positive attitude about it and tried to look forward and not backward at the house that had burned. After my brother's death, I started looking around at what I had to do to get a house built. I took it a day at a time, and I tried to sort through the possibilities and be sure that I was getting what I wanted. I had been born in a log cabin and was raised up in another log house. I'd always loved log houses. I'd always wanted to build one, but I hadn't been able to, or hadn't done it. When my house burned down, everybody said that I should get a trailer. I told them I didn't want a quick fix. I knew that this was my opportunity to build the kind of house I wanted.

When I was trying to decide on the style of log house I wanted, I looked through a catalog of log houses, and then I talked with Charles Wesley, director of Save the Children's Appalachian program in Berea, Kentucky. He'd had the Hearthstone Log Company of Nashville, Tennessee, build a "Cherokee I" house for him, which I liked. I was proud that it had that name, because I'm really fond of the Cherokee Indians. After I examined Charles's house more closely, I decided I didn't want the Cherokee I, because it didn't have an upstairs. When my other house was burning, I couldn't walk in the attic where the fire started to try to put it out. I wanted the model with the upstairs floor, the Cherokee II, so that if anything happened, if there were fire anywhere, I could get to it.

I bought a log structure from Hearthstone Log Company, which came and set the logs. The log structure that was put up was just a big square building. My son, Ralph, and I laid out the space the way we wanted it.

There are lots of local people around here who know how to build, because they've had to build their own houses. I thought if I could take what money I had or could get, I would put it into hiring local community people to work on my house, because there are no jobs around. Besides Ralph, several other people worked on the house: Harold Osborne, a neighbor; Bennard York, my nephew; and some of the women from the day care center. Debbie Lucas, another neighbor, was also very helpful. Another person built my chimney. A church group from Colorado working on a barn with the animal project built my mantle and framed in the fireplace. All my grandchildren helped out, and I did what I could. I did all the buying and all the supervising.

We started building my new house in April 1986, the same month my cousin's husband died. We had to wait until the snow went away and the bad weather got over with. I was moved in by July. Of course, I ran out of money. I didn't want to borrow money and go into debt because I thought that at my age I didn't know whether or not I could pay back a loan. So we just stopped building, because it was nice and comfortable and warm enough. I worked and saved a little bit of money and had the rest of it finished, so it's even better now.

Some more work was done on the house by a group of students from the University of New England in Biddeford, Maine, who took a winter term course in January 1989, coordinated by Nancy Herzberg. The group came to visit my community and stayed in my home for a couple of weeks. The course was called Going Home. Many of the students were from rural areas and were studying for careers in allied health and education. I felt so good about them that it was like a real homecoming.

They wanted to know if they could help me with any special project. We took a look around my house and decided what needed to be done. They went out and purchased materials. Then they built walls to divide the kitchen from the dining room and the dining room from the living room. They built a beautiful hearth around the fireplace, decorating it with rocks and shells they brought from

Maine and rocks I'd collected from here, there, and everywhere. Then they began the long journey back home to apply in their own communities the lessons learned and experienced here about service to people.

There have been so many hands laid on this house that I really dedicated it to the Lord. I paid people to work on the house, but there were so many people who came and did little things that were voluntary or gave me money to help me pay the local people. When it was finished, I said: "This house is open. I'm not having any big 'open house,' but it's open. Anybody who wants to come to my house is welcome." Whoever comes, whomever I work with, has got a place to sleep and my kitchen to cook in.

I've never had all this space, not even as much as I've got on the first floor, and I have a basement too, where the furnace is. I knew I didn't need all the space for me, or for me and my granddaughter or whoever stayed with me. But I thought that if my children or grand-children or anyone else ever lived here, they would have space for a big family. The second-floor space would be good bedroom space. I'd thought about putting a bathroom up there, but with my limited amount of money, I didn't do that; I may some day. It's now sealed and finished, and it's a really nice place. I could have a desk up there if I wanted to. I could go up there to read and study or write. I could also have an area for my sewing machine and sewing supplies.

The upkeep of the house will be very minimal for whoever lives here. Because of the kind of structure it is, you don't have to paint or paper. I didn't want any paint in this house. I can't paint, because I don't like the smell of it. I won't have to do anything to this house unless the roof leaks. I didn't get to put on the kind of roof I wanted. I wanted wood shingles, but I was advised by Charles Wesley that it's really hard to get them on so that they don't leak.

I think my house is beautiful, and it's what I wanted. It came at a time in my life when I can appreciate it more than I would have at any other time. I have a nice living room that opens into the dining room and kitchen; it's comfortable. I love the big, beautiful beams, and some day I'm going to have hanging baskets filled with beautiful flowers and vines. I also hope to have the front of my house covered by roses.

Even when I was a very small child, I had my own garden. My mother was a good gardener and taught me everything I know about gardening. I loved to dig in the ground. I liked to plant things and see them grow, blossom, and produce. Gardening was one of the ways our family earned part of our living. As far back as I can remember, we raised our food and canned it or dried it. We had food for the wintertime, as well as the summer when things were growing.

I still like to grow my own food, my own potatoes and onions and all kinds of other vegetables and fruits. I still love to dig in the ground. There's something about it that really thrills me. It makes me feel so close to the earth and so good about what it produces. Some of my favorite projects are sowing seeds, nurturing them, and then watching the tiny plants burst through the soil and grow and produce. I like harvesting the fruits, vegetables, flowers, and herbs and preparing them for preservation, like drying flowers, herbs, beans, and peppers.

One of my favorite activities is the canning of food for use in the winter months for my own family and as gifts for my friends, neighbors, and staff. I love gathering wild elderberries and black-berries and turning them into beautiful, tasty jams and jellies. I also love going out on the hillsides and gathering wild greens, especially "poke salad," to can and freeze for later use. Other special things I like to make are sauerkraut, pickle relish, mixed pickles, tomato juice, tomato sauce, and chow-chow. Chow-chow is made by chopping cabbage, green tomatoes, onions, and red or green sweet pepper. You add a tiny bit of hot pepper and boil the vegetables in a mixture of half vinegar and half water, then sweeten to taste. One of my favorite foods is corn, which I freeze and can. I also can and freeze vegetable soup made from every vegetable that grows here.

My mother taught us how to can the right way. I've known a lot of people whose canned food spoiled. But we never did lose our food, because my mother would always say, "If you sterilize your jars with boiling water and cook your food well so that it's rolling and boiling, it won't spoil." That was true; we followed that, and I still do. I never lose anything that I can, because I do my canning the way she taught us. I know it's right, because my food is always nice and pretty.

I take pride in canning. When you have your food at home, it's much better, much fresher than what you can buy at a store. You know what you've got. There are no preservatives—maybe a little salt, but nothing that's dangerous—and it's not out of a tin can; it's always in glass jars. It's a real way of life that most people used to know. I've never lost that art. No matter how hard I work or how many jobs I have outside the home, I still raise my garden and can my own food. And I know if I didn't work on a public job, I could eat, and our family could eat.

Around here neighbors will call you and say, "Come and get some peppers, come and get some beans from our garden," or whatever they have. We do the same thing. If we have more than we can use or somebody else doesn't have anything, we always share our gardens. That's a neighborly thing people do here in the mountains. They're not selfish. If they raise something and they're proud they've got it, they want to share it with somebody.

The first autumn I lived in my new home I strung green beans and red and green peppers on thread and hung them from my fireplace to dry. I hadn't had a fireplace to do that before, and it was really special to me. When I was growing up, those were some of the things we always had around our fireplace. We would hang shuck beans, which are green beans strung on thread to dry in the sun. (They're also called hay beans or fodder beans; sometimes they're called leather britches). We also had red peppers strung up, pumpkins drying in front of the hearth, maybe the kettle in the fireplace where we cooked beans or homemade hominy, the butter churn sitting close to the fire to keep it warm. These are traditions that we grew up with and that I really appreciate.

I just love my fireplace. For safety, I put an insert called a Buck Stove in the fireplace, which encloses it. I try to use the wood that's available to heat with as much as possible. I also like to have a little bit of fire to look at, especially when it's cold. It's nice to watch the sparks fly and imagine all the things you can see. It's a cozy feeling to sit by the fireplace and make something with your hands.

Making quilts has been very important to me all my life. When we were growing up, Mama used to hang the quilt from the ceiling on strings. We lived in a very small house, and when she sat down to quilt, it was really hard for the children to get around. We were either under the quilt or bumping into it, causing Mama to stick her fingers with the needle; then we were in trouble. But we grew up with that. After I got married, I usually quilted at my mother's house. Jim and I would put up a quilt and quilt it out; we would work on it together. I didn't like to sew much, because I never liked to sit down and do a lot of things. I liked to be outside doing things. I always needed to be moving.

When I was sick and couldn't get out and do much, I began to do a lot of work cutting quilt pieces. When my legs were in such bad shape that I could hardly walk, I began to try to exercise my legs with the sewing machine. I would sew those quilt pieces together and make beautiful cushions and quilt tops. Some other people have made quilt tops for me, because women needed to work to earn money to help support their families. When I was working and could have a little money to pay them to make me quilt tops, it would help them to have some money. I had lots of beautiful quilts, quilt tops, and pillows when my house burned; all were lost. Even though this would be a great house to quilt in, I've not made any quilts since then, because I've been too busy.

I know it's not just because I'm getting older that I'm so busy. I've not slowed down that much. I've speeded up, if anything. The work is more intense now. The needs are greater. All over the country the economics are such that there's a great need for developing new training programs and new jobs. I don't have time to do some of the things I'd like to do. I've got some pillow tops I'd like to make. I really wanted to make each one of my grandchildren a quilt, but I've not done that, and I probably won't. I might hire somebody to do it someday. I might sew quilt tops together, but I'd have to get somebody else to do the quilting. To take time out from the work I'm doing would not be right; I don't think I'll ever do that. I want to be sure that I don't do things for myself when the Lord has led me to do for others.

STEREOTYPING AND RECOGNITION

People stereotype mountain people because they don't know any better. People believe we are like what *The Beverly Hill-billies* television show portrays us as being, ignorant hillbilly and mountain people. The trend has been for writers and photographers to come and go from our area. They've written books, articles, poems, and jokes. They've taken photographs and made movies about the men and women of the mountains. Many of these people have put us down, representing those who live here as ignorant, lazy, shiftless, and indifferent. This is true for some people wherever you are, but certainly not all.

My people have been put down and shown in a bad light for a long time. We are often shown as being drunk and carrying shotguns. That's not the way we are. Some may have shotguns. I've known of murders and killings taking place, but that's not the way we all are, and that's not the way we should be shown in the movies or in books. For many years, I've been picking up books that have been written about the Appalachian people. I would read a while, and I'd get mad. Many times I didn't finish the books because I didn't like what was said.

The people here are often presented as being uneducated and poor. It's true that a lot of us don't have a good education. But no matter how limited our learning from books may be, every person has something unique to share with others. People are put in castes now and called low-income, middle-income, and high-income. I have a really hard time with that. A lot of us here don't have jobs. We are poor, if you look at what material things we own. But if people would look at the things we can do and what we stand for and the love we have for each other, they couldn't call us poor at all. We would be the richest people in the world.

One woman who came into the area called the women we work with poor. She said, "That's what we're used to calling people when we're up North."

I said, "We don't talk that way down here. We don't call our women poor. We call them intelligent, beautiful, loving women. If you're going to work with our people, you treat them like the greatest people in the world."

When I talked with her later on, she seemed to have changed a lot of her attitudes. She seemed to be getting some education that many never seem to get. The longer people stay in the area, the less they use terms about us loosely.

I also don't like people thinking that you're supposed to act a certain way, that if you're from the mountains, you're supposed to act like a mountain person and if you're from the city, you're supposed to act like a city person. We've had a lot of people, including students, come to our communities to work with us, some volunteer, some paid. One of the things I've always resented was people coming here wearing the worst clothes with patches and the most ragged shoes they could have on. We don't even dress like that. But because of the image that's been portrayed of us, they think they've got to dress that poorly. They want to dress the way so-called poor people do.

When people come here, I don't think they know any better than to do some of the things they do. They may come very innocently, and perhaps they've been told that they needed to do this. Even though people may not know it, we're smart enough to figure out what they're trying to portray. It's very disturbing when an image is set up for you to act or look like.

I have wanted to write something for many, many years to help people understand that just because you're from the mountains, it doesn't mean you're a "mountain person"; you're simply a person. And if you're from the mountains and love them as much as I do, it makes you a special person. I feel I'm much more educated about the area where we live than anybody could be who comes into the area and talks about loving the mountains or loving the land. They may love the issues about the land, but they can't feel the same love as people who have lived here all their lives.

What I want to pass on to my family as a gift and leave with people as I go down the path of life is our belief in ourselves. For people to believe in themselves and have pride, they have to be proud of who they are and of their parents and of the place where they live, even though they may not own a lot of material things. If they can just have that sense of pride, they can overcome almost any obstacle that's put in their way.

If we believe we're as good as anybody else, that what we have to say is worth as much as what others have to say, then we can hold to the idea that we're not different. People are people. We're all God's children. I don't care if we're black, white, red, or brown—none of us are set aside. We're all created equal; we're born equal. There's no difference unless you look for difference.

I've always felt good about myself and the people I was around. I didn't have any sense of being an "Appalachian" person until we began to be talked and written about. Sometimes I've been insulted by the way people have asked me where I was from. I've told them that I'm from the Tennessee mountains as far back as you could have lived. I've always been proud of my upbringing and my experiences growing up in a home where there was so much love that I always felt like a dew-kissed rose each morning when I awoke. I've always added that I think my area is the most beautiful place in the world and that I've never been away for very long.

Sometimes people have asked me, "If you are from this part of the country, why do you talk so differently? Why are you so different?" I've answered that I didn't realize I was. It didn't make me happy that they thought I was different because I don't think I'm that different from anybody else. I've just been able to do a lot of things that others didn't believe they could do.

I have been nationally recognized for my work, not because I was a typical "Appalachian mountain woman," but because of the work I do and what I believe in. Dolly Parton was given a *Ms.* Woman of the Year award, not for being a songwriter and singer or a movie star, but for writing and singing songs about real women and for bringing jobs and understanding to the people of the Tennessee mountains. I was given the honor of presenting Dolly with her award because we have much in common. We are both strong women born and raised in these Tennessee mountains who love our Tennessee mountain homes and our people. We never let stereotyping stop us. We work to make the area a better and more beautiful place to live.

Dolly has written many songs about leaving the East Tennessee mountains to follow her dream; one very beautiful one I recall is "Wildflowers." She left her mountain home to follow her dream, while I have stayed in my mountain home and community to follow my dream and turn it into a reality. Each of our paths has been hard to follow. I know how hard it has been to live out my fantasy by staying in my Tennessee mountain home.

I'd been working for many years, just doing whatever I could. We had come a long way with our ministry. In 1980 the Channel Ten television station in Knoxville was having a contest to recognize people who had not yet had any recognition for their work. I don't watch enough television to know what's going on in the world, but some of the staff had gotten excited about that and nominated me for the Jefferson Award for Outstanding Public Service Benefiting Local Communities. This award is granted by the American Institute for Public Service to people who are doing unselfish things to help others. The staff wrote a little piece about my work and how I'd been instrumental in developing programs that were helping children and helping people with jobs and education. They all signed their names to it and sent it in.

I was out in the garden at the child care center one day when someone came and told me that I was wanted on the telephone. When I came in, the man on the phone said: "I'm Walt Martin from Channel Ten television. You have been chosen as one of five people in East Tennessee to win a Jefferson Award. You were nominated by some of your friends. It's very important for you to be here on Friday with the others who have been chosen." I agreed because I didn't know any better. I was very surprised and didn't know what was happening.

When all five of us got to the television presentation, we were interviewed about our work. We were able to say what we wanted to about what we were doing and how much it meant to us. We were each presented a bronze medallion. They told us that each of our names would be submitted to the national selection committee along with names from all over the country, and that we'd be notified. There would be five chosen on the national level. As time went on, they kept sending me letters saying, "You are sixteenth in the finals," and "Please keep June open for the possibility of going to the national awards ceremony."

Finally they said, "Out of thirty-three thousand nominations, you are one of the five chosen to receive the national Jefferson Award for Outstanding Service Benefiting Local Communities." Channel Ten was still involved, and its staff members were really happy that one of their people was to be given a national award. They said they would fly me and one other person to Washington, D.C., where the awards ceremony was going to be held on June 24, 1980, at the U.S.

Supreme Court building. When I asked my husband if he wanted to go, he said he didn't, but my daughter wanted to go. Channel Ten paid for the flight for Chris and me and all our expenses in Washington and gave me $210 spending money. With that money, I paid for half the air fare for my friend, Virginia Miller, who wanted to go along so she could introduce me to an American Indian woman who was instrumental in getting money to help some Indians here to get jobs. We also went to see some other people in Washington who could help our work.

At the same time we were there, the members of a group called Rural American Women were having a conference at the White House. I had been a board member of this organization for about five years. It was a good way for rural women and women's groups to be heard in Washington and other places throughout the country and the world. As soon as the awards ceremony ended, I went over to the White House for the Rural American Women conference. I was interviewed by a lot of newspapers there.

Getting the Jefferson Award started out as a very lowly little thing with our staff just appreciating what I'd done to the point that they wanted me to be recognized. It ended up giving us some visibility throughout the nation that we wouldn't have had otherwise. I was interviewed by lots of newspapers, among them the *Washington Post*. Many representatives, senators, and others sent me news clippings. National television carried the story. We were then better known throughout the country, and when our name was mentioned or we'd go somewhere, people recognized who we were.

It was a real breakthrough, not only to be honored personally, but to have our work recognized nationally for what it was. Getting the award was a great experience, and it gave me a lot of incentive to go on and want to do more to help other people. I hope that one day some of the people I work with will be recognized as I was for their part in all this work.

A few years later, another woman from East Tennessee was recognized for her work, and I got to play a part. I was totally surprised when someone from *Ms.* magazine called me in 1986 and said: "We've named Dolly Parton as one of thirteen women to receive our 1986 Woman of the Year awards. We are calling to ask you to present her award at our awards ceremony. We're giving her the award, not because she's a country singer or a celebrity, but because she's taken the resources of her success as a country singer and celebrity back to the hills of Tennessee and given jobs to her own people around Sevierville and the Smoky Mountains." That's where she was born and raised.

I didn't know that *Ms.* magazine gave Woman of the Year awards until they called me. The year before I had been interviewed by a young woman on the staff of the Ms. Foundation for Women. She had come down to do a site visit, because we had submitted a proposal to the Ms. Foundation for the maternal and infant health project. I'd shown her around, all over the countryside, and we had had a really good time. When *Ms.* decided they didn't want to find another celebrity to give Dolly the award, this woman said, "I know the very person." Besides our both being from East Tennessee, the reason I was chosen to present this award to Dolly is that I work to try to provide training, employment, and services to the people in my mountain community. I serve people in some of the same ways Dolly does: creating jobs for the jobless, hope for the hopeless, and help for the helpless.

It was very important to me to be recognized as a presenter to Dolly, and I said yes before I even remembered that I was supposed to be in Charleston, West Virginia, that same day to attend an important CORA meeting. I called up the CORA office and said, "I can't be there. I have to go to New York City to give Dolly Parton her *Ms.* Woman of the Year award."

They said: "Oh, go do that. You can't turn that down, because we can wait for you."

I said, "Well, I'll be back to the meeting."

It was a great day for me. I flew up to New York and was met with a big limousine. They had to play it very cool. They said I would recognize the limousine driver they had hired to pick me up at the airport, because he would have a little sign that said, "Ms. Kemplen." I would recognize him, but nobody would recognize me. It was a little different from anything I'd ever done. I didn't have to be under security when I went to get my own award, but with Dolly Parton and some of the other stars who were there, we were under tight security. Anyway, I recognized the man in the airport, and he was very kind.

As he drove me to one of the finer hotels in New York City where the awards ceremony was to take place, he began to talk with me about why I was there. I don't think he even knew that I was going there to give Dolly Parton the award. He said, "I know that you're connected with *Ms.* magazine, but what do you do back home in Tennessee?" I told him, and he got really excited and began to talk about where I might find resources and people who could be instrumental in helping in my ministry. Here was a total stranger wanting to know what I did and offering his ideas for what might be helpful.

Dolly earned the award for her involvement with Dollywood, which has created jobs for low-income people of East Tennessee. Dollywood is a recreational theme park in Pigeon Forge, in the foothills of the Smoky Mountains. It replaced Silver Dollar City, where I had gone many times with children's groups. The schools would always take the children there, because they had things children could appreciate and enjoy, like amusement rides and crafts demonstrations.

When Dolly Parton bought Silver Dollar City, she developed a lot more rides for children and added a lot of country singing. She hired many people to come there and perform. Every few steps you go in Dollywood, there's a group singing or performing in some way. Dolly's kinfolk—her aunt and uncle who helped her become famous, and also her cousins—sing there every day that Dollywood is open. She's not only created jobs for people in the music world but jobs for many other people who work in the park keeping the music going, serving the food, running shops, and doing mountain crafts. Dolly has developed a museum of her own there in a replica of her childhood home. She told me when I was in New York that they had put $6 million into Dollywood in 1985 to make it a better, more attractive place for people to visit. They've added more rides and other things for children to see and do.

I felt really good about being at the awards ceremony, which many men and women attended. I didn't feel out of place at all. I felt I was no different from any of the other women there. We were all appreciating and struggling for the same things. Even when I stood beside Dolly, I felt that we were just women. I spent quite a bit of time talking with her. I met the staff of *Ms.* magazine and the Ms. Foundation and learned to appreciate them in the short time I was there, only one day and one night.

The next morning we were all in the big hotel lobby together, the women being honored and the mothers, sisters, and friends who had come along with them. Only two of the women being recognized had presenters. The rest of the awards were just presented by the *Ms.* staff. I felt as honored as Dolly.

Though I'd never met her in person, I had felt a connection with Dolly from the very early years of her being on television, especially because of her love for the East Tennessee mountains. She used to play on Cas Walker's show when she was a little girl. You could tell by her dress and her ways that she was from the mountains. They always talked about her being from a big family. Her songs were written about her home life and her experiences in the mountains. We came to really appreciate her. I watched her sing and grow up and kind of kept up with where she had gone. I always felt she had left the mountains to pursue her career, but her spirit was always here. She always came back.

Now that she's come back and is making Dollywood a great recre-

Dolly Parton and Tilda at the *Ms.* Women of the Year awards ceremony, January 12, 1987

ational park, going there is very inspirational. During my last visit, a lot of church buses were there, because it was young people's church day. The young people from all the surrounding areas had come to appreciate what's there. I felt really good about it. I feel that Dolly and I will cross paths again and that somehow we're going to have a greater connection.

Here is the speech I gave at the awards ceremony on January 12, 1987:

> Most people in the East Tennessee and Smoky Mountain area could be labeled "poor" if you measure us by the jobs we hold and the material things we possess. But if you measure us by our love for one another and the way we support and treat each other, we are by far the richest people in the world.

Dolly Parton's family was labeled "poor" even by standards of other families living in the same community. Children made fun of Dolly when she wore a rag coat that her mother stitched for her.

Her mother told her the Bible story of Joseph's coat made by his mother, and Dolly wrote the most beautiful of all her songs—"The Coat of Many Colors." It remains her favorite song of the more than three thousand songs she has composed.

I remember when she was a child about ten years old playing her guitar, making up and singing her own songs on Cas Walker's *Farm and Home Hour* to help support her family.

From the very beginning, she used her songs not to conceal or escape her background, but to explain and celebrate it. Just as she refused to let the children make fun of her, she refused to betray her own people.

When Dolly became successful, she brought the talented people of East Tennessee along with her in the road show called the Traveling Family Band. When she became more successful, she opened a theme park to celebrate the talents, culture, and crafts of the Great Smoky Mountains and East Tennessee. That park, called Dollywood, brings millions of visitors and thousands of jobs to a part of America that is as underdeveloped as many Third World countries. We have to respect Dolly for bringing the theme park and an economic development project. Not only has she brought country lyrics and music into mainstream America, but she's also brought the mainstream of America into the country.

With her own unique qualities of style, she has become a very successful businesswoman. With writing and publishing her own songs and making her own records and movies, she has taken all the devalued symbols of femininity and turned them into laughter and power, making millions of us proud to be women.

Dolly, you make all of your natural and spiritual kinfolk in East Tennessee proud and empowered. Because you are honest, strong, and proud, you have turned most of America into Dolly's kinfolk.

On behalf of all of us who see you as our symbol of beauty, strength, courage, inspiration, and hope, I am proud to present to you this award as *Ms.* Woman of the Year, and I am especially proud to be your neighbor in East Tennessee.

Four

From Roots to Roses

The following was presented to me by Alex Petterson, a Danish man who helped parents in Campbell County set up a center for the developmentally disabled in the early 1970s:

CERTIFICATE OF APPRECIATION
Awarded to Tilda Kemplen who "Saw the Light"
It is few who see, realize, and understand that the past and present only exist because of the future, and that no one of them is more than the other. Therefore, the seed planted in the past must be cared for in the present to bear fruit in the future.

This is the first time in my life I've ever really reached back inside myself to see why I am as I am. I had to begin by thinking about my childhood days, the most important time in my life. I've never lost sight of any of the beauty I experienced as a child. My love for the beauty of the earth and what it produces—the flowers, the trees, the berries, and other food—gave me a magic carpet to start out on. Recognizing the beauty around me gave me the vision to want to do the things I've done. I wanted to create a situation where a person can become like a flower popping up and creeping out of the ground to bloom into full beauty and become what the Lord intended it to

151

be. The beauty of everything is so much more real to me now, and it gets better and brighter all the time.

My view of God is that He dwells within me. It's not something out yonder. He's in everything. I see the glory of God in every blade of grass, every leaf on a tree, every flower. I can see His handiwork in the spider web and in this web of life that we're all working on weaving. The Supreme Being creates us and keeps us. This Higher Power stays with us if we only recognize Him. He teaches us if we allow Him to.

As far back as I can remember—and I can remember things from back when I was two and three years old—I always wanted to do something more than it seemed I was able to do. I had a vision of something that was higher and bigger than I was. It seemed that an "all-seeing eye" was always on me. I felt there was great work for me to do. I knew as I went along that if I just waited and followed my feelings, God's divine power would guide my life and help me become what I wanted to become.

I've allowed God to direct my life, and I feel good about that. I know that it has to be His love that keeps me and helps me to be what I want to be. I believe that everything I've done and everything I'm going to do the rest of my life is in a plan that is just falling into place. I believe that God looked down through time and saw everything that He intended me to do. I only had to be willing to be led by his unseen hand and lean upon his everlasting arm for strength, faith, and courage to step out and do his work.

All my life I have felt that God has had a real place for me and that God has a real place, a real mission, for every person born. I feel that we are what we are, not by our choice. We had nothing to do with our being men or women. We all have jobs to do. Each of us has a ministry to do that is ours, and nobody else can do it. Nobody has the same truths and beliefs as mine or holds the love that I have. No one else can have the vision I have or do things the way I do them. I don't feel I'm any better than the next person, but I can be proud of who I am, where I live, what I do, and what I stand for, no matter how poor I am or how poor I've been, no matter how many things I have or don't have—I don't need many. I'm just proud to be here.

It may not seem like a great ministry to many, but I would rather be able to say a kind word, wear a friendly smile, or give a drink of water and a piece of bread to someone in need than to own all the riches this world can provide. I feel very strongly that when you're able to help someone else and are willing to share whatever you have with others, you are helped much more than they are, because it makes you feel so good inside about who you are and what you can do. I believe that each of us is charged with loving and caring for one another in whatever way we can.

When I began talking about developing a comprehensive creative learning center, someone commented: "What can you create? Only God creates." That's not what I believe. I know God creates us and every living thing and gives us the spirit, the wisdom, and the knowledge to do creative things, like sprinkling the nutrients on the root system to turn it into a beautiful rose garden. As the saying goes, I'm a "co-creator with God."

This spirit has helped me to help other people recognize their own talents and realize that they want to have a better education, be better teachers, better parents, better students, or just better citizens. I've always told people that I know from experience that you can be what you want to be. When you have that Higher Power watching over what you're doing and are directed by the spirit that's within you, there aren't enough other things to stop you. People can do a lot more than they believe they can. I've found it's not hard for people to believe that—once somebody says to them, "You can do whatever you want to."

I've always had the vision of trying to help people become what they have the potential to become. I've stressed the importance of education, self-esteem, and self-motivation. I've offered people chances to go places they might not otherwise have visited and opportunities to meet people. I pride myself on being able to make others feel good about themselves by encouraging them to do things they may not have thought they were able to do and telling them what a good job they do. I've tried to help them realize that they, too, play a great part in all we do, that their part is just as important as mine in making the things happen that we want to see happen, such as the services, the education of people, and jobs.

I've seen a lot of people who work with me get really excited about where they are and what they are doing. As one of our staff members has said: "That's why I've stayed with the organization I'm with. That's why I've stayed with the job I have. We may be led, but we're never pushed back or pushed around." That made me really happy, because to be a leader doesn't mean suppressing people. It means helping them become whatever they desire to be. I've seen people come from not even knowing who they are to being very knowledgeable about themselves and their role in life.

It's not been hard for me to encourage people to realize that their talents and their work can become a reality to themselves and to others. They in turn may lead ten others toward their goals while never losing sight of where they have come from and who they are. I think there are people who do lose sight of where they have been and who they were before they became successful in making things happen. I never lose sight of who and where we are as I lead and guide people.

I feel that when you have a vision, you have to be guided by that vision to reach your goal in life. Having been born under the sign of Aries, I've been blessed by being directed toward a great vision. What I see is a big picture. It's like a big picture puzzle. There are always parts being put in place as we reach toward our goal. But unless we keep on reaching, it would be finished, and we wouldn't have that goal to work on. I think a lot of people might finish their puzzle. I have never gotten the last piece in place, because I've never stopped reaching.

As we get one thing finished, we take a step further and build on it. The need is already there, but we cause it to surface to the point of people taking hold and trying to make it become a reality. I've been accused by my staff of being able to dream up more than everybody could do, which is true, and I like that. I do think of things that can be done, and I think far beyond where we are every day. I try to never leave anything unfinished unless there is someone ready to take on the task.

I'm not doing things by myself. I encourage many others to come along, and sometimes they go on and do things and get way out ahead of me. For any project that I can develop, I have no problem with people walking along beside me who will soon take it on as their project, directing and managing it. This is especially true of the women I work with. They take on a project and make it work. That's the way I like it. I do things with people, but I don't want to do things for people. I'll do anything for anybody if they need me to, but as soon as they're able to take on that responsibility, I want them to take it. All they need is an opportunity and someone to show an interest in what they believe in and are trying to accomplish.

The most beautiful relationships grow out of the experience of people working together. Sometimes in the evening I get phone calls every five minutes for a whole hour, many of them from members of my staff. It is of great importance to me to hear the voices of my coworkers on the other end of the phone line. They're really excited about what they're doing. We always have a lot of projects going on, and they want to tell me about the things they have done that day and to ask where I think they could be of greater service the next day.

Sometimes I have to be gone all day to attend meetings or look into possibilities for developing more jobs in our community. I think the staff misses me when I'm gone. What they want is approval and encouragement to go on and do a better job. I need to encourage the staff so they can go out and encourage other people to feel good about themselves and join in things like the education classes and other activities that are going on.

It really encourages me when I see other people taking on responsibilities. They don't wait for me. They may wish I were there sometimes or may call me later to tell me what has gone on during the day. But they are taking hold of the situation and making it work. That makes me really happy, because if I were the only one doing things, or if they were waiting for me at every turn, there wouldn't be a lot done, and my work would sort of be in vain. I know that my dreams will never die, because so many people are beginning to dream and work to make their dreams become reality.

I always try to encourage people to feel in control of their own situations by doing things they thought they couldn't do. One day, Evelyn King (a long-time member of the day care staff) invited me down to videotape her family reunion and become part of it.

I said, "I want to be in some of the pictures."

When I handed her the video camera and showed her how to use it, she said, "I might as well learn, because you're going to see that I use it."

I said: "Yeah, you're going to use it. I'm not the only camerawoman around. I can carry that old camera, but I'm not the only one who can use it."

When Evelyn saw that she could work the camera, she was really happy that she was filming her own homecoming, and she began filming me along with her family. I like to show people that I'm not selfish with what I can do. I want them to do it too so they can carry on, because I never know what new thing I'll want to do tomorrow.

When I get to feeling there's something I have to do, it opens itself up like a rose opening its petals. It may come by way of a child. It may come by way of somebody calling me and asking, "Can you do this?" or "What can we do to help you?" It may open up a whole new school of things, a whole new package. It might be a job development project or an educational activity or something else that needs doing. I may not have thought of it before, or maybe I'll be thinking of the same thing as someone else at the same time. I won't ever forget when Nancy called me in 1986 and said that she'd had this revelation that she just had to come help me with this book, because she and I had talked about it back in 1974. At the very same time, I was getting geared up to do it.

You must allow yourself to be guided, and you must have patience. I've had to learn to have patience. I didn't always have it. Timing is very important, and I've learned in the last few years that there is a time for everything. I always knew that, but I never waited on anything. I was always out there trying to do things, maybe trying to make them happen before their time. In the last few years, I've learned that things do happen at a special time. Sometimes we try to put things together out of season, and they just don't work. Then all of a sudden the time is right, and the work falls into place. It has to be the right time, not just for me but for the people I'm working with. Right now, the time is right for a lot of things to happen, and they are happening.

My role has been and still is to help other people see that my vision has led me to do something about the needs in our communities. People have to dream and not daydream. When they see that they need to be doing a certain thing, they need to do it. If we all work together, there is strength in numbers of people. But I don't think it takes a lot of people to make important things happen. A few people who think alike and believe the same way and believe in each other—that's what really makes things work. We need to take whatever vision we have and find ways to make it become a reality. Sometimes it's not easy, but by just keeping on we certainly can make a difference.

I always try to speak the truth about our area, and I try never to say anything that would put the people down. I always say that the people are not to blame for not having an education, and they are not to blame for not having jobs or having good houses. Their problems come from the place where we live and the way things have been in the coal industry, which was never owned by the local people. They had no control over what happened in their lives until they stepped out and began to make decisions about the problems and issues that affected their lives and the communities in which they lived. It is very important for people to stand up for what they want, regardless of whether they can get it. If we would all stand for a cause and stand together, there could be a mighty big change in the valley. But I've found that most people will not stand proud on issues that are controversial.

I've experienced from a long time ago that for every good thing we try to do, there is always something to block it. I've always gone straight ahead and never quit when somebody tried to hinder my efforts. There are always stumbling blocks. I have said many times: "You don't have to step on anybody or go over the top of them when they become your stumbling block. There are many ways around." You just take the other way around and go in another door. I've had to take a lot of side roads and detours to keep from bumping into things or hurting somebody in the process. The stumbling blocks cannot stay in your way if you try to do what's right, because there's a great unseen hand that removes them at just the right time. I have never let anything keep me from doing what I thought was right. I just keep on going, and if people don't like it, that's their problem; I don't have one.

People who try to hinder development don't understand. I've thought of the song I love so much, "The Rose Among the Thorns," about how roses have to live and die among the thorns. Sometimes people would like you not to do the things that really make you show up as someone who helps people to be better off by helping themselves. Sometimes people would like you not to do things that create change or make a difference.

At first, hardly anybody except a few special people believed in many things we were trying to do. Some of the people with power and money could have done something about the situation, but they didn't see why people like us were trying to do something in a rural area where it was unheard-of to serve children or the elderly or the sick. Some people in high places think that they're highly educated and that they know it all. It's really hard to convince people that you're going to do something whether they help you or not. I use this phrase quite often with people, including those in the highest agencies and others who hold the power in their hands: "If you help us, we'll do it, and if you don't help us, we're going to do it anyway."

I feel, as I have felt for many years now, that I have been and still am a missionary. It's really hard to be a missionary in your own community among your own folks. I try to walk along with all the local people, though I know that people get a little leery when you go and do things that people normally don't do, like going to college or going to Washington or wherever else you need to go to make an impact. They don't know where this all comes from, where it all fits in.

Some people are jealous and don't want to see you doing things that maybe they could do if they tried. When you're a person from the community where you've grown up, people don't believe that you can do certain kinds of things, and they would like you not to be able to do them. If you go ahead and do those things, they try to get in your way. Sometimes they put out false rumors and say things that aren't true; they may think they're true, but they're not.

From Roots to Roses

I've learned that the only way you get anything done is to do whatever you start out to do, regardless of what obstacles get in your way. Sometimes people won't step over even the smallest obstacle to do the thing they want to do. But I would climb the highest mountain of obstacles to get over them and prove to myself and others that it can be done. When we stand up for what we believe in and don't give up on anything, people learn that we're going to do things and that nothing they say or do is going to make any difference to us. They might try some things to block us, but pretty soon they'll get out of the way. They will actually begin to help when they can fully understand that we're trying to make our communities better places to live and rear our children. Those who come to understand what we're doing say: "That's why we appreciate your work so much. That's why it's growing and spreading all over the world."

In our work we talk about the weaving of a web, and I would never want to put a snag in it that might cause it to unravel. I think of the title of Jesse Stuart's book about his teaching experience, *The Thread that Runs So True*. I feel that there's been a thread running through my life and work, and I want to keep on weaving, along with community people. I feel very strongly that local people—those I grew up with, those I've helped raise, and the children coming up today—need to be in charge of their own communities. They need to be able to take charge of their own lives and not be too influenced by anybody unless they believe in what that person is saying. They must never step off their principles to gain someone's friendship or sell their votes for somebody's dollar.

For almost every project or program ever done by the people I work with and myself, we didn't have anything to start with. We didn't have any money. We didn't have a building. We started out with zero everything, so we couldn't go anywhere but up. All we had was ourselves and our dream. Our work has slowly but surely taken root and climbed to great heights. If I had a lesson to teach people, it would be to start with whatever they have, wherever they are, and work with whomever they can—whether a very small child or an older person—wherever they are in their way of life and their way of thinking. That's what you build on.

When you put yourself into something, it works. I feel that to take a vision and turn it into reality, you have to dedicate your life to it. When people ask me how to set up a child care center, I ask them if they have a person who would dedicate their life to it as I have. If they say that somebody is interested, I ask if they are interested enough to give up everything they have to make it work. Even if they are interested themselves, they don't know. They would like to see it happen, but they don't know how they would make it work. It's not that real to them.

I have a hard time with people who are trying to do some of the same types of things we've done without being totally dedicated to the communities and to the people. I hate to see people half-committed. One of the things I try to teach is that if you care about something, you've got to really care. We use the phrase, "A degree of caring is much more important than a degree from college." If you can read and write, and if you have love in your heart for people and can dedicate that caring toward what you're doing, you'll be a success. You have to have commitment, total commitment. To me, commitment means that if I'm going to try to do something, I'm going to give it everything I've got to make it work. Nothing is going to make me turn away from it if I believe in it. Even with a million dollars to put into projects, they wouldn't work without commitment. The million dollars would soon be gone, and there would be no base for the ministry.

You have to believe in something enough to commit yourself first. Even with small things, like raising money to help a sick person, if you commit your own dollar first, then other people will come along and commit their money to it. But if you go out with an empty plate or an empty hand and say, "We want some money from you," it doesn't work. I've experienced from a long time ago that if I could put mine in first, if I committed myself, then other people would commit themselves.

When I dedicated my life to the work I'm in now, it was long before I started creating a child care center. It was when I began trying to get to where I could teach school so that I would be in a position to help children. When I started college, I gave it all I had. I didn't drop my family by the wayside to do my college work. I pulled them along with me so that I could do it all at the same time. A lot of other people will say they can't go to college because they have children, and I say: "That's just not right. You can go if you've got children, and your children will appreciate it." My children very much appreciated the fact that I went to school, even though it made it hard on all of us.

You have to dedicate yourself so you get yourself out of the way of progress, because you can be your own worst enemy. If you put yourself into something to the point that you can't be the enemy, then others can't keep you from doing it. People can be their own worst enemy by putting themselves down and making excuses: "I can't, because I don't have any money" or "I can't, because I've got children at home" or "My husband wouldn't like it if I did that." What you're doing is talking to yourself, and you really are your worst enemy when you don't do what you're able to do and when you don't believe in yourself.

So I don't have any excuses to make. And I can make a split-second decision like snapping a finger. I didn't have to think twice when Nancy said she wanted to come down to work with me on this book. When I was called to go and give Dolly Parton an award, I agreed in a second. These are the kinds of decisions I can make, because I'm in charge of my life.

I try to keep a very simple way of life and a simple but powerful way of thinking about things. I have this small voice that lets me know right from wrong. There are two simple, important things: right and wrong. Politics, religion, and other things that confuse most people don't confuse me at all, because I don't let them. I do what I think is right, and I don't try to get over in left field if somebody over there looks a little better or talks a little better or a little louder. I try to think about what's right for me, what feels right in my heart.

One time a young woman asked me what I thought about foot washing in the church. She told me her church was talking about doing that, and she didn't know how to think about it or what to do. I told her that the church I go to down in Georgia does that.

I've been there and it's beautiful. Everybody participates, including the children. To me, it's an act of kindness, of caring enough about your neighbor to do whatever Jesus himself would have done. I said: "Think about it as service. If your church is going to do it, think about whether you want to be part of it. If in your heart it feels good and feels right, and it's beautiful to you, then it's all right." I didn't know what else to say, but what I'm getting at is that I follow whatever feels right to me.

I believe a lot of people get confused because they don't trust their own judgment. You must speak the truth as you believe it or know it and not let anybody confuse you to the point that you don't know whether you're right or wrong. I think that if you're guided by the power and the spirit that's within you, you don't have to get too concerned about what people over there are saying or doing. You've got to be true to yourself, first of all. I believe that the biggest problem people have is with their own identity and their self-respect and self-esteem. If they don't feel good about themselves, they can't be true to themselves. There's a lot to be taught and a lot to be done to help people understand themselves. Everything that's important to them has to come from inside.

People seldom realize that they have this inner strength, this inner person they have to deal with. Others can't give me much except friendship and love. I've got to have something within me that sustains me and keeps me true and honest. I need to be true to and honest with myself and believe in myself enough that I know what's right to do. Otherwise it would be really hard to live with myself. I'm the last person I have to deal with in any situation. When I go to bed at night, I'm the last person I talk to and reconcile with and the first person I have to deal with when I wake up in the morning.

I've steered away from the people who predict things that are going to happen. A lot of people get really concerned about what's way out in the future, and they get confused about things that are beyond their control. I don't worry about what's out in the future. I tell anybody I'm with, "Do what you can do today, right where you are." Every morning when I wake up, I just thank God I'm still here. When I go to bed at night, I think toward the morning. I don't think about yesterday, unless I'm thinking about some things that have happened that guide me on to the next day.

When I was a child, I wanted to be a missionary. I thought from everything I'd read that you had to go off somewhere like Africa or Asia to be a missionary. That was confusing because I couldn't go. Then as I grew a little older and saw what I could do and how much need there was in the field of service to people, I understood that "mission" means working to help people wherever you are. You don't have to go anywhere.

Somehow as I grow older, my ancestry, my heritage, my roots all seem to be much more important to me than they've ever been in my life. I see other people feeling the same way. They seem to appreciate the simple life they've lived, their American Indian heritage, their grandparents, the stories of the older people. I think people need a real start in life by having a place they can put down roots and be proud.

In the last few years, a lot of people have come back to the mountains from places where they tried to fit in but couldn't. And there are people who didn't go anywhere but still don't fit into their own communities and the schools, churches, and organizations that are around. They just don't seem to know where their place is in this great nation of ours, and that's sad.

It all goes back to the need for having a home and knowing where you belong and what belongs to you. What people need is an opportunity to do things for themselves and do things with others that can make them feel they're an important part of their community. It gives them stability to have a place where they belong and something they can contribute. They can serve one another. I once heard someone make the statement, "Every person should be able to look into a mirror and see a hero." Very true.

It's important to have a place in the community or in the school or church that you feel good about, because you have to live in the physical world. You have an inner person, but you also have the outer person who has to fit into society. Whatever that society is and wherever you are, you need to be counted and to count yourself as a person who is really important in that community, school, or church.

The schools and churches and whatever clubs and organizations that are going on in a community sometimes leave a lot of people out. Some of the people who get left out could be the most instrumental in making things work, but because of class or family, they get left behind. I try to lift up those people whom other people don't feel too good about. Over the years, I've seen children who didn't feel they fit in, especially at school. They were just there. I tried hard to make each one of them feel important by giving them important jobs to do and working on their interest level, whatever it was. Children need to get started in the right direction. I want to instill in children the feeling that they are special and have special talents, that they're beautiful and can always do whatever they want to do. If children feel good about themselves, they will take a place in their community if they're allowed to.

When I see children who are happy and laughing and dancing and carrying on as they do every morning at the day care center, that is glory enough for me. Those little children's faces seem like a whole bed of flowers that have bloomed because of love. My desire to help them be better off and to help them appreciate the beauty of life grows from within my heart. It's a real process of love, truth, honesty, and beauty. It can't be spoken; it is felt and can only be expressed through deeds of kindness and love. By this time in my life, there are probably thousands of people, both children and older people, whose lives I have touched and who have touched mine. We're all better off for it.

I've been trying to create something beautiful out of the past. To use something like Alex Petterson's phrase, I've tried to take the past and bring it forth into the present so we can have a future. I'm really happy about being as old as I am now, because up until this time I would not have been able to reach into the past the same way I can now, bringing it into the present and making it work with what's going on so that it can bring a brighter and more beautiful future for everyone, especially the children.

We talk about our children being our greatest resource, and I can't get away from that. If those of us who are older don't leave something with the children to be proud of and to treasure, we won't have a future, and they won't have a future. So that's what I'm struggling for, the future of my children, grandchildren, great-grandchildren, and others too. The root of all our work is the children, starting with the yet unborn children. When you start with the children, you can't go wrong, because you can't do anything but go forward.

The people who work with us in the child care center and in the other programs are mostly women. The women are often just like the children when they come to work. For a few days, they may be those tiny rosebuds, and then suddenly you see them becoming very happy, opened up and in full bloom. Then they're able to do whatever they need to do, like talking with anybody who comes by. Soon they're ready to go with me wherever I want to go and do whatever is needed. We've gone many, many places to speak, including county court meetings and churches. It's something they never believed they'd do.

Over the years we have seen the young women as well as the older ones become very backward and nervous about going on a job, maybe for the first time. I guess they didn't know what to expect. One time we had a beautiful, intelligent young woman join our staff.

She said: "I'm so nervous about starting this new job. I got so excited last night about it that I tossed and turned all night."

When she came into work with a dress on, I said, "It's awfully cold to have a dress on."

She said, "I thought if I got dressed up, I wouldn't be so nervous."

I try to spend a great deal of time with the women, making them feel good. We try to tell them: "You don't have to be nervous here. You don't have to be upset. Just come on in and become one of us."

I feel strongly about how the system of development works, how the work grows from one person to another, how people are blossoming and maturing to the point that they feel good about themselves. Somehow we're not planting a seed that's in such shallow ground that it doesn't grow. The depth of our work is like the root system I've tried to describe many times. I see a system, a root system, that's very deeply grounded or rooted underground.

I like to think that what we do is something that's going to last forever. Maybe a house won't last forever, but the love people have for that house or the love they have for a garden will last. The garden is going to be gone after that summer. But the appreciation they've developed is going to last forever, and it's going to keep on blossoming and producing that good feeling in people.

I've heard the term *grass roots* so many times that I don't like it, and I don't use it much. When I hear people use it loosely, I think they're just using it as a term to talk about something that doesn't have any roots. I like to think about economic and community development and the development of people as being more than grass roots. There are tree roots and briar roots, things that really have some stability to them. The roots are much deeper than grass.

As we put down roots in any kind of development situation, they grow and then spring up in another community, in another person, even in another town, another city, another country. I've seen our work grow by leaps and bounds, but it's not the kind that comes from the top down. It comes from the heart of Mother Earth. It's that kind of thing I see happening with people that makes me so happy.

In my imagination, I see this beautiful root system, like a giant oak tree standing somewhere with all the roots going out far and near. As a shoot springs up through the ground in the spring of the

*From Roots
to Roses*

167

year, it's like a person beginning to bud and blossom. Then it begins to make something happen wherever it is. That root system is
something I've been looking at and thinking about for a long, long
time. If we're grounded in our work and if we really believe in it,
we'll make things grow and blossom from roots to roses.

From Roots
to Roses

1. Speech to the Commission on Religion in Appalachia

The following is a talk given by Tilda Kemplen to the CORA assembly on September 23, 1988, in Weston, West Virginia.

> I will lift up mine eyes unto the hills, from whence cometh my help. My help cometh from the LORD, which made heaven and earth. —*from Psalm 121*

Yes, we will lift up our eyes unto these once beautiful Appalachian mountains that were graced with the beauty of hills, hollows, streams, valleys, and gullies by the great hands of the almighty God. These mountains have been and still are home to most of us. I grew up loving the mountains, feeling a sense of great strength, shelter, and safety in them, but sometimes now we look unto them for strength and beauty and see only ugly scars made by man, and stripes like the face and body of Christ when He was here.

These mountains produce and retain a rare breed of strong, honest, caring people who have been and still are exploited by people who come into the area to save us, educate us, research us, and write about us, trying to keep us dependent upon missionaries, welfare, food stamps, and handouts in order to keep us poor and ignorant. I am one of these mountain people. I have gone to college, and I am what I am by the grace of God. I am proud of who I am.

If I have a sermon to preach or a lesson to teach, it is to be proud of who you are and of what you can do and to stand for what you believe in. Have a set of standards to live by and principles to stand on and never step off as long as you believe you are right. And always seek divine guidance.

For the assembly this year we have chosen the theme, "What Difference Does It Make?" I would like to begin with what a difference it does make when we care and join our hands in Christian fellowship and our hearts in Christian love and service. We can surely make a difference. To care we have to know; to know we have to see, hear, and feel the hunger, anxiety, the hopeless feeling of not having jobs to be able to support our families; of being sick and unable to get medical care; of being unable to read to our children, to read the newspaper or the Bible; of never owning homes where we can feel a sense of ownership and be in control of what we do. Until we can be in control of our homes, get an education, and have jobs, we cannot be in control of our lives or put down roots that can anchor us in self-control, hope, faith, courage, and self-worth, so we can become the full-blossomed roses that God intended us all to be.

I challenge us in the CORA family to look, see, listen, feel, and hear. If we have ears, let us hear. If we have eyes, let us see. If we have hands, let us use them to do God's ministry here in these mountains. If we have feet, let us use them to walk about this great land to see, hear, feel, and serve. If we have a heart, let us use it to love and to care; let us keep it so clean that hatred, envy, jealousy, greed, deceit, and malicious pride have no place in our lives. God gave us hearts that we might love each person, great or small. Now let us keep this heart so clean that only love can grow.

If we have a voice, let us sing God's praises, but let us speak out loudly and clearly when we see injustice. Let us speak softly to children, friends, neighbors, fellow workers, and our enemies. Let us speak kindly about one another always and remember how much more we can do to make a difference if we are in harmony and unity.

If we have a mind, let us use it to learn. To learn what? Perhaps that we need to do for others and not for ourselves. To learn to read so we not only can read to someone, but help them learn to read. To learn to work and grow food so we can give a hand, not a handout, to those less fortunate than we by helping them learn to grow their own food. To learn not how to get a job for ourselves and be happy, but to help others prepare themselves and get jobs so they can have hope and self-esteem. To learn not so we can look down on people, but to humble ourselves to help them grow and exceed our level. In this way, we find what our purpose for being here is.

Let us never use our gifts and talents to beat down, but to prop up and raise up those who may not have the same gifts that we have. Let us never, never forget for whom we are trying to make a difference.

2. Tilda Kemplen's Education and Teaching Experience

1931–40 Attends grade school.

1957 Enters college at Lincoln Memorial University.

1959–61 Teaches at Fonde Elementary School in Bell County, Kentucky.

1961–62 Attends college full-time for half a year to complete degree. Teaches one-half year at Henderson Settlement Elementary School in Bell County.

1962 Graduates from Cumberland College with a B.S. degree.

1962–64 Teaches at Upper Laurel Fork Elementary School in Bell County.

1964–66 Teaches at Fonde Elementary School again.

1966–67 Teaches at Finis Ewing Elementary School, Tackett Creek, Campbell County, Tennessee.

1967–68 Teaches at Primroy Elementary School in Campbell County.

1968–69 Begins the school year at Primroy school, then is transferred to Wynn Habersham Elementary School in Campbell County to teach the slow learners.

1969–70   Teaches slow learners at Wynn Habersham Elementary School.

1970   Attends Tennessee Technological University and the University of Tennessee during the summer and earns an endorsement in special education.

1970–75   Teaches at Wynn Habersham Elementary School.

1973–present   Teaches for Mountain Communities Child Care and Development Centers: adult education, including basic education (reading, writing, arithmetic) and arts and crafts; high school classes for dropouts; and child care and preschool child development classes.

3. The Evolution of Mountain Communities Child Care and Development Centers, Inc.

1967   Organization of child care program begins.

1968   Summer recreation programs begin for children of all ages in the White Oak, Tennessee, area.

1969–73   Recreation programs operates for children of all ages in six communities.

1973   MCCCDC incorporates.

1973   Child care center starts in single-wide trailer.

1973   Adult education program begins.

1973   Food and clothing distribution programs begin.

1974   Double-wide trailer for the child care center is purchased.

1979   After trailer burns, present site is purchased and operation of the child care program begins at this site.

1979	Library is established.
1979	Solar greenhouse and gardening project begins.
1982	Native Herb Products operation begins.
1982	Maternal and Infant Health Outreach Worker Project begins.
1985	Mountain Communities Livestock Project begins.
1986	Toddler program begins.
1986	Emergency food pantry is established.
1987	VISTA literacy project is established.
1988	Drug and Alcohol Abuse Prevention Program begins.
1988	Child Abuse Prevention Program begins.
1988	Free-standing greenhouse is built.
1988	Eighteen acres of land is purchased.
1989	Mountain Communities Small Farms Program begins.

Suggested Readings

Appalachian Heritage, a quarterly publication of Berea College, Berea, Kentucky.

Carawan, Candie, and Guy Carawan. *Voices from the Mountains: Life and Struggle in the Appalachian South*. Urbana: University of Illinois Press, 1982.

Couto, Richard A. *Streams of Idealism and Health Care Innovation: An Assessment of Service-Learning and Community Mobilization*. New York: Teachers College Press, 1982.

Gaventa, John. *Power and Powerlessness: Quiescence and Rebellion in an Appalachian Valley*. Urbana: University of Illinois Press, 1980.

Jackson, Melba. *Indians to Interstate: A Book About Caryville*. Jacksboro, Tenn.: Action Printing, 1986.

Page, Bonnie M. *Clearfork and More (History and Memories)*. Clinton, Tenn.: Clinton Courier-News, 1986.

Porter, Eliot. *Appalachian Wilderness: The Great Smoky Mountains*. With Natural and Human History by Edward Abbey. New York: Ballantine, 1973.

Southern Exposure, a bimonthly publication of the Institute for Southern Studies, Durham, N.C.

Stuart, Jesse. *The Thread that Runs So True*. New York: Scribner's, 1949.

Taylor, James H. *A Bright, Shining City Set On A Hill*. Edited by Elizabeth Sue Wake. Williamsburg, Ky: Cumberland College, 1988.

Woodward, Grace Steele. *The Cherokees*. Norman: University of Oklahoma Press, 1963.